STATEMENT OF RESPONSIBILITY

The Committee for Economic Development is an independent research and educational organization of over two hundred business leaders and educators. CED is nonprofit, nonpartisan, and nonpolitical and is supported by contributions from business, foundations, and individuals. Its objective is to promote stable growth with rising living standards and increasing opportunities for all.

All CED policy recommendations must be approved by the Research and Policy Committee, a group of sixty trustees, which alone can speak for the organization. In addition to statements on national policy, CED often publishes background papers deemed worthy of wider circulation because of their contribution to the understanding of a public problem. This paper has been approved for publication as supplementary paper number 251. It also has been read by members of the Research Advisory Board, who have the right to submit individual memoranda of comment for publication.

While publication of this research study is authorized by CED's bylaws, its contents, except as noted above, have not been approved, disapproved, or acted upon by the Committee for Economic Development, the Board of Trustees, the Research and Policy Committee, the Research Advisory Board, the research staff, any member or advisor of any board or committee, or any officer at CED.

Library of Congress Cataloging-in-Publication Data

Timpane, P. Michael, 1934-
Business Impact on Education and Child Development Reform:
a study prepared for the Committee for Economic Development /
by P. Michael Timpane and Laurie Miller McNeill.
p. cm.
Includes bibliographical references.
ISBN 0-87186-251-4: $11.00
1. Industry and education–United States. 2. Education–
Economic aspects–United States. 3. Educational change–
United States. 4. Child development–Economic aspects–
United States. I. Miller McNeill, Laurie.
II. Committee for Economic Development. III. Title
LC1085.2.T56 1991
370.19'316'0973–dc20   91-3828
                                      CIP

First printing in bound book form: 1991
Printed in the United States of America
Design: Rowe & Ballantine

COMMITTEE FOR ECONOMIC DEVELOPMENT
477 Madison Avenue, New York, N.Y. 10022
(212) 688-2063

1700 K Street, N.W., Washington, D.C. 20006
(202) 296-5860

CED RESEARCH ADVISORY BOARD

CONTENTS

FOREWORD

Education has long been a key concern of CED's trustees. As our interest in U.S. economic competitiveness intensified in the early 1980s, CED began to examine how the nation's system of public education was serving our society and our economy. In the past several years, we have issued three major policy statements addressing various aspects of this issue: *Investing in Our Children: Business and the Public Schools* (1985), *Children in Need: Investment Strategies for the Educationally Disadvantaged* (1987), and most recently, *The Unfinished Agenda: A New Vision for Child Development and Education* (1991). During this time, CED has also conducted numerous meetings, large and small, with business, education, and community leaders throughout the nation to focus attention on the needs of children and education.

One result of CED's efforts in this area has been a remarkable growth in the level and sophistication of business involvement in both education reform and child development issues. Yet, as our work in this field has matured, the members of CED's Board of Trustees felt that a scholarly analysis of CED's impact on education reform would be helpful in guiding our future efforts.

In 1988, CED commissioned P. Michael Timpane, president of Teachers College, Columbia University, to conduct a two-year research study on the results of nearly a decade of education reform activity and the impact that business has had on the reform movement. The resulting research report, *Business Impact on Education and Child Development Reform,* provides a critically needed perspective on the involvement of corporate America in the resurgence of public education. The report's authors, Dr. Timpane and Laurie Miller McNeill, research associate at Teachers College, note that while there is a long way to go to achieve the nation's education goals, many of the initiatives currently being implemented are promising in their range and scope and are symbolic of a new commitment to develop the nation's human resources to their fullest.

In this effort, the impact of the business community has been significant. The business role has evolved from early "helping-hand" relationships that emphasized partnerships between individual businesses and schools to a more substantive role in leading coalitions for reform and initiating policy change at the state and national levels. The study examines the many different types of initiatives in which business has taken part and provides a framework for future business involvement.

Although its views are entirely those of its authors, the report provides strong support for CED's efforts to develop sound and practical recommendations on education and child development policies. As a work in progress, the study contributed significantly to the research base for CED's 1991 policy statement *The Unfinished Agenda.*

We are deeply grateful to Dr. Timpane and Dr. Miller McNeill for the insight, experience, and intellectual expertise that have made this paper such an important contribution to our understanding of the issues. I also wish to thank the Chairman of the CED Subcommittee on Education and Child Development, James J. Renier, chairman and chief executive officer of Honeywell, Inc., and the subcommittee members who offered helpful guidance in the development of this volume. My special thanks to Sandra Kessler Hamburg, CED director of education studies, for her superb editorial guidance.

Finally, we gratefully acknowledge the many private and corporate foundations, listed on page vi, whose generous support made this publication possible.

This volume is being made available by CED as a framework for addressing the many concerns relating to business involvement in education and child development reform. It does not contain specific policy recommendations and in that respect differs from CED policy statements, which contain recommendations developed and approved by CED's Research and Policy Committee. *Business Impact on Education and Child Development Reform* provides a fundamental and constructive perspective for ongoing consideration of the future direction of education reform and the important role that business can play in bringing that about.

Sol Hurwitz
President
Committee for Economic Development

ACKNOWLEDGMENTS

We wish to thank the CED Subcommittee on Education and Child Development, particularly its Chairman, James J. Renier, for its thoughtful comments on the earlier drafts of this paper that helped to strengthen the final product. Harold H. Howe II, Marsha Levine, Sue Berryman, and David Bergholz also offered helpful comments in their reviews; Linda MacKenzie provided invaluable research assistance; and Nancy Griffing edited and produced the report's many drafts. We also extend special thanks to CED President Sol Hurwitz and Sandra Kessler Hamburg, director of education studies for CED, for their guidance, support, and editorial expertise throughout the research and development of this project.

Finally, we would like to thank the members of the CED Research Advisory Board who reviewed and approved the final draft for publication: Astrid E. Merget, acting dean, College of Business, The Ohio State University; Richard N. Rosett, dean, College of Business, Rochester Institute of Technology; and Thomas C. Schelling, distinguished professor, Department of Economics, University of Maryland.

P. Michael Timpane
President
Teachers College,
Columbia University

Laurie Miller McNeill
Research Associate
Teachers College,
Columbia University

We wish to give special thanks to the following foundations and companies, whose generous support made this publication possible.

Aetna Foundation, Inc.

Carnegie Corporation of New York

The Edna McConnell Clark Foundation

Kraft General Foods Foundation

Charles Stewart Mott Foundation

PREFACE

The renewal and expansion of business's interest in education and child development programs during the past decade has been an occurrence of great and growing scope, variety, and significance. It will be many years before we know its full extent and its impact on the education and adult lives of our children. It is not too soon, though, to try to analyze the context and causes of this activity, its patterns of development, interim accomplishments, and major obstacles and limitations. This is what we have tried to do in this study. In the process, we have drawn on several sources: the knowledge we have both gained during several years of personal involvement in the reform movement, a review of the extensive literature listed in the Bibliography, the staff resources and records of the Committee for Economic Development, and over fifty interviews, mostly by telephone, with business, government, and education leaders who have been deeply involved in state and local education reforms during the 1980s.

We, like many, are disappointed with the slow progress in some aspects of educational and child development initiatives advocated by business leaders and education reformers. But the enterprise under way intends to reinvent schools for the twenty-first century, not to give education a face-lift. Those who expect education and public policy to respond to their demands with businesslike precision underestimate the scope of the changes being advocated, the complexity and time-consuming nature of institutional change in education, and the democratic processes governing our schools.

Furthermore, the success of the school reform movement must ultimately be judged by how well these endeavors improve schooling. Whatever reform accomplishes in this regard, it will not feed hungry children, house homeless families, reduce federal or state budget deficits, offset the weakened financial sector of the economy, or single-handedly restore communities disrupted by economic change. There is an established but frequently misguided tradition in this nation of seeing schools as the cause of and solution to myriad problems. As we go about the important business of education reform, we must be realistic about what it can and cannot accomplish.

In our judgment, the contemporary business involvement in education has so far been substantially beneficial. But it can only be part – and a supporting part at that – of the solution to education's problems. These problems are, in our estimation, rooted in the nation's lack of a strong belief in the need for and possibility of a good education for everyone (our rhetoric to the contrary notwithstanding) and the consequent lack of sufficient political will to produce the excellence we say we seek. This is a problem for all the people.

INTRODUCTION

The United States has begun a new era of public policy and private action to provide the knowledge our citizens will need to keep our nation united, free, and prosperous. There is a new commitment to the development of all our human resources for these purposes as we once again recognize the interdependence of government, education, and business. Although there is clearly a long way to go in order to achieve the kinds of reform now advocated, new coalitions are being built to forge consensus among diverse groups and to conduct the important debate about the purpose of education and schools.

In the words of former New Jersey Governor Thomas Kean, the process under way involves nothing less than "reinventing the school for modern times." But even this expansive assessment may underestimate the changes that will be needed, for the times demand new approaches to early childhood development and a new emphasis on the education occurring outside the classroom and indeed throughout the life span of our population. As states and localities consider how to invest funds most efficiently to assist their people, there is a growing recognition that policies concerned with education, social services, and economic development must be viewed as parts of a whole rather than as independent choices. This nation has embarked on a difficult and important new task: redefining its commitment to its citizens, especially its children.

One of the most dramatic and significant aspects of this decade-long process has been the rise of private business interest in education reforms and improvements, the reassertion of a historical interest interrupted during the 1960s and 1970s. This resurgence was the result of a new analysis of the needs of business today and of the ways in which those needs should be integrated into the nation's broader social and educational requirements. Arising from dramatic changes in demographics and the general economy (and labor markets specifically), this analysis was soon extended to the application of new management theories and new perceptions of accountability to the world of education and recently to an emphasis on early intervention for poor and disadvantaged children. The most forceful and influential expression of these views is found in two Committee for Economic Development policy statements, *Investing in Our Children: Business and the Public Schools* (1985) and *Children in Need: Investment Strategies for the Educationally Disadvantaged* (1987).

Business's interest has been manifested in a wide variety of education programs and policies and has persisted, expanded, and changed throughout the decade, becoming more appropriate and effective with time. The scattered and marginal school-business connections in the early 1980s were thought to be negligible. Yet, these partnerships, seen initially as temporary phenomena, developed swiftly and surprisingly into strong and widespread business support of school-level projects and help for school district and community enterprises. Business also spoke with a new and confident voice in local, state, and national policy councils. In each of these realms, its efforts are as energetic in 1991 as they were in 1985.

To be sure, business interest and involvement in school reform have not solved the problems of education. Business projects in local schools still vary widely in scope and effect and often barely address, let alone provide, needed improvements in the larger education system. Opportunism often persists among the school-business partners, even as they gradually gain understanding of each other's enterprise.

The education policy developments of the 1980s have strongly reflected the interest of business in education reform, producing three distinct types of initiatives consistent with the business agenda: (1) improving educational quality by raising standards for students, teachers, and schools and focusing on accountability; (2) restructuring schools as places of work and teaching as a profession; and most recently, (3) focusing on the educational and social service needs of at-risk children through the provision of early childhood programs and greater coordination between educational and social services.

These different emphases involve different kinds of activities in different arenas. Efforts to set new standards for learning and accountability have gone forward principally in state capitals, with governors and other officeholders leading efforts to develop explicit new education policies. School restructuring is ultimately a local affair, without uniform prescriptions for the difficult job of redesigning the organization of work and learning in individual schools and school districts. Addressing the enormous educational and social service needs of at-risk children involves interinstitutional and interagency collaboration of unprecedented magnitude among social welfare, education, and health care services. Business leaders have found it more difficult to participate effectively in these endeavors as they progress from policy making to restructuring to collaborative service systems.

The legislation and model programs produced so far are only the beginning of a national movement toward greater accountability, empowerment of teachers, and restructuring of schools. And mistakes have been made. Some efforts to improve accountability that have enjoyed business support have been inappropriate attempts to codify complex expectations for the educational process, with no connection made between expectations about what students should learn on the one hand and how they are taught and what resources are available for the process on the other. In other cases, rhetorical support by business and education leaders at the national level for early intervention initiatives has encountered considerable skepticism at the grass roots and has led to little action. Different states and localities have moved at different speeds in addressing new agendas. Nevertheless, an impressive amount of creativity is being applied to some of the most difficult problems of education. There is a growing commitment to education and child development reform, along with the creation of exciting new ways of approaching some of this nation's thorniest educational and social service problems. Educators, businesspeople, and legislators are settling in for the long haul in educational improvement.

Among the most significant changes taking place are in the ways educational policy is made. At the state level especially, there is a new politics of education. In most states, the initiative in setting education policy shifted during the decade from state boards of education, chief state school officers, and educators to governors, legislators, and business interests. New mechanisms for the development of policy have been discovered: special task forces and commissions that emphasize the involvement of business. States have struggled to achieve greater coordination among education, employment, economic development, and social welfare policies. Education has topped state policy agendas almost every year for a decade. State education politics will never be the same.

A new politics of education is also evident in some urban centers. In cities such as Boston and Chicago, business leaders have played a major role in defining and executing the education reform agenda. High on the business agenda in those cities were new structures for decision making and governance – such as school-site management and school governance councils made up of parents, teachers, and principals – intended to alter permanently the politics of education in their communities.

In these processes, we can see both the possibilities and the limitations of the role of business in educational reform. Business can help define problems and provide advice, encouragement, and support to educators and policy makers, but it cannot effect policy reform or improve schools. These must remain public responsibilities.

If there is any bias in this report, it is toward optimism. Ten years ago, debate about public education centered on how to cut public spending in what was thought by many to be the most ravenous branch of the public sector and on how to circumvent the perceived shortcomings of public school education. Today, there is a nationwide debate under way in the education profession, in legal forums, in corporate boardrooms, in state capitals, and at the national level about the purpose of education and about the things that must be done to support and strengthen all schools and teachers. Only two previous debates in public education have rivaled the current one: the debate at the turn of the century about how to design a system of publicly supported mass education and the debate from midcentury on about assuring equal educational opportunity, treatment, and results.

CHAPTER 1

THE ORIGINS AND CONTEXT OF BUSINESS INVOLVEMENT IN EDUCATION

The involvement of business in education is not new. For the first half of this century, industry in America was a strong force behind the movement for universal schooling and for vocational education. Most school board members were business or professional men, and public school management came to be modeled on business management. Business and educational leaders agreed that the preparation of students for a productive work life was an important objective of education. Curricula, testing, counseling, and placement programs all developed within this comfortable consensus. The last chapter in this early history of business involvement in the schools was the prodigious expansion of the public schools after World War II.

The context of educational policy making changed swiftly in the middle and late 1960s. Though the change was most dramatic in the cities, it was also evident in communities of every size throughout the United States as new issues of educational equity, due process, and political power came to the fore. And with those new issues came new actors: organized parent and community groups, organized teachers, advocates of previously neglected groups of students, lawyers and judges, and federal and state program managers. These new issues and groups were unfamiliar and frustrating to the businessmen who thought themselves stewards of the schools. For the first time – in issues such as desegregation, busing, and school violence – business leaders confronted the possibility of real costs in their participation in educational policy, and they began to pull away from service on local school boards and the like. Over a period of only a few years, business's influence was eclipsed, and its representatives were less and less prominent in the deliberations about local educational policy and rarely involved in the development of important new state and federal educational roles.

Thus, in the critical years from the mid-1960s to the late 1970s, business interests became increasingly distant from the schools, shifting toward the universities. The children of business leaders often attended private elementary and secondary schools or public schools in elite suburbs. Lacking contact with the public schools, many business leaders found it easy to believe the stereotypes about public education circulating during these years: test scores falling and school systems failing because of unruly students, untested innovation, militant and uncooperative teachers, and ineffectual administrators.

During those years, too, there was an ample supply of qualified entry-level workers to be found among the large numbers of young people born during the postwar baby boom and among women reentering the labor market. Business could ignore or postpone its concerns about the quality of the schools and concentrate instead on their cost in taxes. Those were the days of strong business support for state tax limitation statutes in California, Massachusetts, and elsewhere, as well as opposition to local school bond issues. Business dealt with schools through the lower levels of its public affairs or personnel offices, which had little authority, small budgets, and as a result, little or no credibility with or influence on educators.

A SEA CHANGE

In the late 1970s and early 1980s, this picture began to change. In cities such as Minneapolis and Dallas, and in states such as California, Florida, and Mississippi, business leaders began to reestablish connections with public education. This phenomenon spread quickly to many other cities and states. And the business community found unexpected allies in education reformers, who were drawing new and far-reaching conclusions from their own failures and frustrations in the 1960s and 1970s, and in a new generation of political leaders, state governors in particular, eager to make economic development through educational improvement a centerpiece of their programs.

What happened to renew business's interest in education? It seems clear that changes in labor supply and demand have been the most significant spur to this renewal. Neither an abstract devotion to the importance of schools in society (to prepare employees, citizens, and consumers), nor local interest in communities that were "good places to do business," nor even contemporary theorizing about corporate social responsibility had been sufficient to rekindle that interest, but a growing concern about the quantity and quality of labor was.

It was a certainty that fewer young people than needed would be entering the labor market during the remainder of the century; the number of high school graduates would decline by 20 percent between 1980 and 1990 and would not grow throughout the nineties. In addition, the proportion of women in the labor market would never again rise as swiftly as it had in the recent past. Spot shortages of labor were beginning to occur, and many industries began to contemplate the need for painful choices: raising entry-level wages, substituting technology for labor, or exporting jobs to new locales here or overseas. The business community realized that with the need to fill existing jobs already apparent and more complex jobs on the horizon, it could no longer afford numerous educational failures in the schools.

Thus, the quantitative issue was quickly joined by concerns about quality. Concern had been growing for a decade about our economy's failure to maintain historical annual advances in productivity. There were many macroeconomic and managerial explanations for this lag, but there was also a legitimate, if unproven, concern that the observed declines in educational performance were being translated into lower productivity in the workplace. This concern was heightened by the decline in the U.S. international competitive position during the 1980s compared with that of Japan and Germany, for instance, whose education systems were efficiently geared to serve vigorous economies.

Yet another factor was the rapidity of technological change, led by computers and telecommunications. There were indications, again unproven, that as the new technologies became more pervasive in the workplace, workers would require different and often more complex skills.

These basic concerns about quantity and quality grew throughout the decade as other changes in the labor market also became more apparent:

- Increasing mobility of the work force

- Increasing heterogeneity of the work force, with the proportions of African-Americans, Latinos, and recent immigrants growing steadily and presenting new educational and performance problems

- Evidence that success in the world economy would increasingly depend more on the quality of workers than on financial or natural resources

All in all, during the 1980s, the issues of human development and performance rose to first place among the concerns of corporate leaders throughout the nation.

The dominant themes of business's interest in education were historical and familiar: management, accountability, and education for work. Yet, their specific meaning had changed dramatically. Education for work no longer meant job-specific preparation primarily through vocational education; it now meant general knowledge and skills that would enable workers to perform in a variety of situations, adapting to a rapidly changing workplace. And it implied special concern for the youngest poor children, who would need more help before and beyond their schooling to attain the necessary levels of literacy and skill.

Similarly, the admonition to education to be "businesslike" had acquired radically different implications. Schools should not be factorylike organizations run by a managerial hierarchy. Rather, they were being asked to restructure themselves, as many large businesses had, in order to give operating sites (i.e., individual schools) clear expectations, incentives, resources, authority, and ultimately, responsibility for producing a greater educational outcome (i.e., measurably improved student performance).

THE CED REPORTS

Investing in Our Children and *Children in Need* crystallized the new business sentiment and were catalysts in helping to create a persistent business involvement in educational reform and improvement.

Until 1985, there had been no comprehensive, widely influential statement of business's interest in education. This interest had begun to burgeon at the local level in the first school-business partnerships and programs of assistance to individual schools and teachers. At the state level, businesses had begun to participate in the development of educational reforms, sometimes on their own initiative and more often at the request of governors and legislators. At the national level, *A Nation at Risk* (1983) gave strong emphasis to the economic and competitive aspects of educational performance; concurrently, in *Action for Excellence,* the Education Commission of the States' Task Force on Education and the Economy (comprised of politicians, educators, and business executives) developed an initial statement of the corporate interest in education. Through all these efforts, there were common substantive threads: a concern about employability and productivity and a conviction that strong academic content, high standards, a focus on outcomes, and clear accountability were the necessary first steps toward educational improvement.

CED was ideally situated to take on the dual tasks of crystallizing and advancing the new business interest in education. As an organization of business leaders and educators, it was able to lead authoritatively. During the previous quarter century, it had made progressive and influential commentary on America's educational and social problems. In 1959, CED published *Paying for Better Schools,* followed in 1968 by *Innovation in Education: New Directions for the American School,* which criticized the increasingly bureaucratic and impersonal character of schools and urged individualized programs. Then, in 1971, it published *Education for the Urban Disadvantaged: From Preschool to Employment,* a report foreshadowing many of the perspectives found in *Children in Need.* Although CED published no new report on elementary and secondary education for the next fourteen years, it contributed a substantial body of commentary on related issues: welfare reform, job training, health care, housing, urban policy, and corporate social responsibility.

In the 1980s, with this unique body of informed commentary to build on, as well as a spirited leadership, an eager membership, skillful staff assistance, and readily complicit colleagues from the national vanguard of education reform to call on, CED took a leadership role in enunciating a corporate vision for the nation's schools.

As is the case with most influential reports, *Investing in Our Children* and *Children in Need* synthesized views already widely held – about economic requirements, employability, education standards, outcomes, and accountability. In addition, by using the compelling metaphor of investment, now widely adopted in a variety of policy contexts affecting education and children, they helped change the nation's way of thinking about the cost of education. Wise investments that yield excellent returns are the hallmark of successful businesses. What had been seen as a cost of doing business now became an essential component of the suggested education strategy: Invest now to achieve benefits and savings later on.

These reports also advanced radical suggestions for bringing about the needed changes in education policy and practice. *Investing in Our Children* was among the first of the national reports during the 1980s to argue for new professional roles and rewards for teachers and "bottom-up" strategies for school improvement. It owed much in this regard to the views of education reformers such as Sizer and Goodlad, but it reinforced their arguments through analogies from contemporary business practice. It preceded and influenced subsequent statements in the same vein by the Carnegie Forum (*A Nation Prepared*) and others.

In addition, the CED reports directed the attention of the nation to the distinctive and growing needs of the youngest, poorest, and most disadvantaged of our children, the so-called at-risk population. Ironically, the voice of business was the first to be heard clearly on this issue, too. One of the early fears about the education reforms suggested with business support in the 1980s was that they would aggravate the problems of poor children in schools by ignoring inequities and the social causes of failure and that they would rely instead on inappropriate standards and measures, looking for quick-fix solutions. Instead, *Children in Need* contains the decade's most influential assertion that the youngest and poorest students are those whom the nation most needs to help build productive lives for themselves and society. In its emphasis on early childhood programs and comprehensive social service approaches for children and youths with multiple disadvantages, it goes considerably beyond the agenda that the business and education communities forged together just a few years earlier.

Finally, CED has been extraordinarily effective in disseminating its ideas and perspectives. Both reports have been distributed in unprecedented numbers and used often by educators and policy makers to stimulate public debate and promote subsequent proposals for reform. CED's leaders, notably Owen B. (Brad) Butler, have effectively carried the word to policy makers, business leaders, educators, and the public. A thorough media campaign stimulated several hundred articles and editorials, not simply reporting but embracing the CED perspective with scarcely a critical word. The most recent expressions of the corporate viewpoint, including the National Alliance for Business's *Blueprint for Business on Restructuring Education,* the *Business Roundtable's Participation Guide: A Primer for Business on Education,* and the statements of the recently formed Business Coalition for Education Reform, are wholly consonant with (and, indeed, derived from) CED's earlier analyses. They are eloquent indications of the success of CED's own investment in children.

EMERGING CONCERNS

By the end of the 1980s, moreover, it was becoming evident that broader economic developments and business concerns were complicating the program of educational reform. The continuing difficulties of international economic competition and domestic public finance and the increasing prospect of recession were reducing the likelihood of sufficient funding for all public enterprises, including education. Persistent changes in the nature and structure of employment and lagging real wages, particularly for younger workers, were helping to expand the ranks of the poor and near-poor, worsening income distribution, putting steadily greater strains on parents and families, and reducing the rewards of educational achievement.

In the face of such fundamental social and economic concerns, education reform will undoubtedly struggle in the decade ahead to retain the momentum so recently achieved, and the strength and durability of business support will be sorely tested, too. Difficult economic times will make advocacy for public spending more difficult and unlikely. Impatience and frustration with the slow pace of educational change and improvement may grow. Current hopes for public school reform may be reduced or abandoned, leading to new pressures for choice or other market-oriented devices as panaceas rather than reasonable policy improvements. In the worst case, current hopes for public school reform may be reduced or abandoned. In short, the business community must continually summon up educational vision and leadership in the next decade as it has in the last.

CHAPTER 2

PATTERNS OF BUSINESS INVOLVEMENT

The past decade has been one of remarkable growth in the number and strength of new alliances among business, schools, and communities. New relationships have been formed at every level of government and in almost every area of educational policy. An entirely new context for educational policy making has emerged, along with a new set of expectations for the role of schools in our society. Government and business leaders have begun to play a new and vital part in deciding the fate of public education. There is an important debate under way in this nation about the purpose of education and an expectation that this debate will be public and that business will play a prominent role in it.

Leaders of business, government, education, and civic organizations are impressed with the unforeseen impact business has had on the education reform movement and optimistic about the benefits it will produce.

To be sure, not every instance of business activity has been substantial and productive. Many so-called partnerships are superficial and likely to remain so. But in many other cases, there is a clear pattern of business involvement in education, a pattern that is often sequential for the involvement of specific firms and progressively more significant to education reform and improvement.

The pattern has gone from a few projects to many, from marginal programs of assistance to participation in efforts to change schools and school districts, and from local to state-level involvement to emerging efforts to shape national attitudes and federal policies.

The stages of school-business relationships are as follows:

- *Helping-hand relationships,* in which business provides tangible goods and services to schools (such as equipment, donations, mini-grants, tutors, speakers, and special materials)
- *Programmatic initiatives,* in which business is involved in attempts to change and improve one particular school or one particular program

- *Compacts and collaborative efforts* providing a single, communitywide umbrella for a wide range of school-business and school-community activities and, in one way or another, pressure for districtwide school reforms
- *Policy change*, where business leaders and organizations have been active participants in developing a vast array of new policies, especially at the state level

HELPING-HAND RELATIONSHIPS

By all indications, the most widespread and popular type of relationship between business and the schools is the helping-hand relationship. These relationships are usually suggested by educators and provided by businesses to supplement or enhance existing school programs. They provide resources the schools could not secure on their own, such as guest speakers, equipment and computers, business employee-volunteers, and mini-grants to teachers. Many adopt-a-school programs, especially those that respond primarily to a wish list of donations developed by schools, begin as helping-hand relationships.

These local partnerships are far and away the most numerous and popular form of connection. They occurred in 17 percent of the nation's schools in 1984 and 40 percent today. There are now more than 140,000 partnerships in 30,000 public elementary and secondary schools, and over half of these relationships (52 percent) are between business organizations and the schools. Small business firms sponsor about 40 percent of the partnerships, while medium and larger firms support roughly 30 percent each.

How successful are helping-hand relationships in promoting school reform or improvement? They are highly successful at achieving peripheral goals. They do not reform education. Branded as "feel good" partnerships by some critics, these relationships do not set out to challenge the ways in which schools go about the business of education or the ways in which business goes about its involvement with schools. Nor do they attempt to redesign a specific program or school or challenge the basic assumptions that underlie the way schools work or the priorities educators set. In the worst case, they are a union of opportunists – both seeking public relations gains.

At their best, though, helping-hand relationships have substantial benefits. Enterprising educators can put the resources that helping hands provide to excellent use to enhance ongoing school programs. IBM's extensive local partnership programs show the breadth and extent such projects can have. IBM involves more than 10,000 employee-volunteers in more than 750 partnerships between its local offices and their community schools. These helping- hand relationships include Join-A-School, Junior Achievement, loaned executives, and mentoring programs, as well as support for programs promoting literacy and education in mathematics, science, and engineering. Support comes in the form of guest instructors and speakers, teacher training, tutoring, equipment, software, participation on special education committees, and advice on curriculum and instruction, management, and school governance issues, among other means. School people are accustomed to scarce resources, and their ability to develop creative projects with limited resources would impress the most economy-minded businessperson. A single computer donation in the hands of a creative school staff can make a significant difference in the day-to-day business of teaching and learning.

Moreover, they often provide a first, safe step toward greater business involvement and allow both the business and the school to get to know each other and form a relationship for the future. When helping-hand relationships succeed, the business interest clearly evolves from "how can we support this school?" to "how can we support more substantial, long-lasting change in education?"

As one southern business leader said:

> Adopt-a-schools and partnerships are O.K. for helping out individual schools and classrooms, but the trend is for business to move to a higher level of involvement. Don't just give fabric for the school play or donate $1,000 for computers; push for reform. Establish coalitions that can contribute to substantive change. Business can help their local school districts create the conditions for social and political change that provide the basis for policy changes school boards need to make....

Business has become more tough-minded, as well. "A few years ago, we gave the schools money, got our picture taken, and shut up. Now we are saying, if we pay — and we do pay through taxes even without the contributions — we want a say in it."

By this route of involvement and reflection, businesspeople become more serious about their involvement in education and begin to work toward the improvement of specific programs, entire school districts, and state and federal policies.

The expansion of helping-hand relationships has been accompanied and stimulated by a decided shift in corporate contribution programs, with corporate giving to precollege education growing almost 50 percent between 1987 and 1988 alone. Many companies report new long-term commitments to precollegiate education, including a new philanthropic focus and direct involvement in schools. Several of the nation's largest corporations have recently dramatized this shift. General Electric has set aside $20 million to double the number of disadvantaged college-bound youths in communities where its manufacturing activities are concentrated, IBM has designated $25 million for innovative computer use in schools, and RJR Nabisco recently promised $30 million for local educational improvement projects.

School people at the local level often have a more cautious, limited view. They see school-business relationships, not as opportunities to undertake far-reaching reform, but as opportunities to foster school-community relations and introduce new resources into their schools. Principals (the most aggressive solicitors of school-business relationships) stress the tangible, material outcomes they hope school-business partnerships can produce. They would prefer to see more awards, scholarships, and special incentives for students; donations of more computers, equipment, or books; the provision of guest speakers and demonstrations; and the use of business facilities and equipment – rather than greater business involvement in the consideration of education programs and policies.

WHAT KINDS OF PARTNERSHIPS DO SCHOOL PRINCIPALS WANT?	
1. Awards, scholarships, or incentives for students	52%
2. Donations of computers, equipment, or books	45%
3. Guest speakers, demonstrations, use of facilities or equipment	39%
4. Academic tutoring of students	33%
5. Assistance for students with special needs	26%
6. Grants for teachers	23%
7. Professional development for school staff	23%
8. Work-study or summer employment for students	19%
9. Special awards for teachers or schools	16%
10. Loan of employees to teach	11%
11. Service on education committees or task forces	6%

SOURCE: National Center on Education Statistics, *Education Partnerships in Public Elementary and Secondary Schools* (Washington, D.C.: U.S. Government Printing Office, February 1989).

PROGRAMMATIC INITIATIVES

Programmatic initiatives represent the next stage of business involvement: intensive efforts to improve one particular program or one particular school by concentrating a variety of special resources on it from both school and business partners to create enhanced learning opportunities for students. They are larger in scale and more complex than helping-hand relationships. They require greater commitment from both business and the schools and a shared vision of the desired outcome of the relationships. They are also the projects that are producing the greatest gains.

There are many varieties of programmatic initiatives, from special science and technology programs in elementary and middle schools, to career-preparation and job-readiness programs in high schools, to reorganization of school curricula. Some adopt-a-school projects are programmatic initiatives to the extent they aim at changing educational practice, as are some management programs developed particularly for school administrators.

Programmatic initiatives differ from helping-hand projects in that they use business resources to change existing practice, rather than to enhance existing school programs. Because of their careful design and the close and sustained relationship between business and the schools, programmatic initiatives tend to produce substantial educational outcomes.

Academies, mentoring programs, and management programs for administrators are among the most prominent and promising programmatic initiatives.

Academies are usually "schools within schools." They combine academic coursework with career preparation and employment opportunities in special fields for high school students. Typically, the programs target economically disadvantaged students in grades 10 to 12 at risk of dropping out (but not those who have already done so). School districts and businesses together create the programs, with a community-based group sometimes acting as a broker. Academies create special learning environments for students both inside and outside school and involve businesspeople in curriculum development and on their governance boards.

The first academy programs were developed in Philadelphia over twenty years ago. The most comprehensive and widespread efforts under way are in that city and in California. Philadelphia currently has academy programs in applied electrical science, automotive and mechanical science, business, horticulture, and health. California currently provides support for eighteen academy programs in areas such as electronics, health, business, and computers and technology; fifteen more are in formation. In New York, American Express began an academy of finance in 1982 and has since added academies of travel and tourism, public service, and manufacturing sciences. These are now expanding under the National Academy Foundation, supported by several corporations and serving 3,500 students in sixty-one schools and twenty-six school districts nationwide. Academies can also be found in Pittsburgh (the Business and Finance Academy in Westinghouse High School), Portland, Oregon (the Financial Services Academy in Jefferson High School), and many other urban centers. Altogether, there are, at most, a few hundred of these initiatives, compared with the many thousands of less ambitious collaborations.

Academy programs cost more to operate than the regular school program ($490 more per student in Philadelphia and $750 more in California), but they are producing significant long-term benefits by improving student achievement, preventing dropouts and unemployment, and increasing college attendance for their students.

Other well-established programmatic initiatives support career development directly. Long present in the schools as an offshoot of vocational education and manpower training programs, these programs expanded in the 1980s to involve the business community in program development and support and to reach more students earlier in their education. New York Working exemplifies this new shape of things. Created and subsidized by the joint action of New York State, the city's schools, business, and foundations, New York Working has set up Career Development and Employment Centers in sixteen high schools, providing career perspectives, academic and employment skills, and job development and counseling support for the predominantly disadvantaged students of these schools during and for one year after high school. Programs such as New York Working intend to be new but integral parts of the schools they serve and to focus on success in matching students with good jobs, using every available community resource.

Mentoring is a more recent programmatic development. Extraordinarily popular with participants, students, and schools, mentoring programs are growing rapidly in numbers – in colleges and universities, community and youth-service agencies, as well as business. There are surely several thousand such efforts, reaching unknown thousands of individual students. Mentoring is based on the simple belief that many students can gain much academically, professionally, and personally from a consistent and caring relationship with a mature adult. If comprehensively implemented in a school, a mentoring program can ease the school-to-work or school-to-college transition, enhance job readiness, target troubled and at-risk students, or help tutor students in their schoolwork. Some mentoring programs, such as General Electric's College Bound Program, combine one-on-one volunteer mentors with other school improvement strategies. Others involve collaboration with civic leaders, college student groups, retired persons, and parents.

How successful are mentoring programs? It is far too soon to know. One recent study of elder mentors paired with at-risk students found that well-designed programs do indeed have an important impact on youths. Powerful bonds develop between these young people and their mentors that, according to a study by Public/Private Ventures, "help change a life trajectory from one headed for failure to a more adaptive path of survival." The youths involved reported important qualitative improvements in their day-to-day lives. The mentors, in turn, "took on the youths' full range of problems and emotions," helping the young people through crises, acting as their advocates, and bolstering their sense of stability and competence.

On the other hand, studies now under way suggest that the costs and other difficulties of mentoring programs involving businessmen and women have been underestimated by their enthusiasts. Mentoring must be viewed at present as a hopeful, albeit popular, experiment.

Business can also change schools by *management development* and *administrative analysis*. Some of the earliest instances of the new business interest were of this nature (e.g., in Chicago and Minneapolis), and some of the most recent initiatives (e.g., in Denver) extend the practice. Some projects admit school administrators to corporate management development programs: Bell-South sends school principals to Outward Bound-type training; Procter & Gamble trains teachers and principals in Cincinnati, as does Xerox in Rochester and throughout Virginia. Pacific Telesis and Wells Fargo send management educators into schools in California. In other instances, businesses loan executives and other staff members to work on special assignments in schools and share business techniques with school leadership.

Addressing management development needs has been a particular priority of the Partnership for New Jersey's work in education. The organization, which represents the leadership of New Jersey's major corporations and selected nonprofit institutions, supports two programs of this sort: one that pairs administrative teams from individual school districts with a corporate sponsor and one that works with the state's department of education to provide management development opportunities to educators throughout the state.

Management Assistance for Public Schools (MAPS) is the older of the two programs, pairing participating school districts with a single corporate sponsor for a two-year period. Four to five days a year of corporate management training are provided to school district administrative teams in subjects such as conflict resolution, problem solving and decision making, team building, communication, and management and leadership. The program, now entering its fifth year, encourages corporate-school district partners to go beyond the initial focus on training and the two-year commitment.

To be effective, such business involvement must be sustained over a period of time and directed toward administrative teams rather than individuals and must carefully adapt business methods to the public school setting.

COMPACTS AND COLLABORATIVES

Compacts and collaborative ventures differ significantly from programmatic initiatives and helping-hand relationships. They are not relationships between one business and one school; rather, they are joint efforts involving several businesses and one school district. Rather than investing in one program or one school, compacts and collaborative efforts coordinate a variety of efforts serving a number of programs and schools, as well as fostering districtwide policies geared to school improvement and reform. Civic and community organizations, higher education institutions, and local government are often included in the efforts. By organizing under one umbrella, business and community leaders become an important force for districtwide school improvement and reform. A unified coalition supporting an agenda for educational improvement and reform dramatically alters the context for educational decision making in any community. It creates new forums for debates about goals and performance and new expectations that district education officials cannot ignore.

The compact and collaborative efforts established over the past decade have varied greatly. Some coordinate existing activities; others challenge district and board policy on school improvement and reform issues. Both are important demonstrations of business and community involvement in the schools, but they embody two different strategies for change. Compacts and collaborative efforts that are primarily coordinating mechanisms provide community and business support for *internally* driven school improvement efforts. The relationship is primarily supportive; it fosters school improvement by supporting programmatic initiatives and helping-hand relationships with the district.

Local education funds (LEFs), which have been created in several dozen communities, are prominent examples of this type of collaboration. They bring business executives, community leaders, and school managers together to develop and provide resources for an array of supportive projects. Mini-grants for teachers and community public relations assistance for the school system have been the projects most frequently launched. In the larger efforts, such as those in San Francisco, Los Angeles, Pittsburgh, and New York, the LEFs have also supported extensive professional support for teachers in the arts, sciences, mathematics, and humanities; dropout-prevention programs; and local models of educational reorganization and improvement.

Compacts and collaborative ventures that are oriented toward political action create effective *external* pressure groups to drive school reform efforts. The relationship can be adversarial, at least to the extent of forcing the scope and pace of change.

Implicit in these two strategies are competing philosophies about what is wrong with schools and what should be done to fix them. Those compacts and collaborative ventures that emphasize supportive strategies (programmatic initiatives and helping-hand relationships) advance the view that school programs need *improvement*, something that can be brought about partly by extra resources and moral support provided by business and community leaders. In supportive relationships, business and community groups work cooperatively with school officials on targeted areas to bring about improvement.

In case after case, these extra resources make an important difference in school programs, often providing that extra measure needed to make sure students are exposed to new opportunities for learning. Most of the early collaborative ventures were of this variety, with Pittsburgh's Allegheny Conference Education Fund serving as the exemplar. In Denver, for example, the Public Education Coalition sponsors a wide variety of projects, supporting teaching training to improve students' literacy skills and providing management and efficiency studies for school management, mini-grants for innovative classroom projects, education forums for community leaders, and a campaign to inform the public about important education issues. The Cincinnati Youth Collaborative targets four areas: instruction, preschool, the school-to-work transition, and leadership development for district teachers and administrators.

In contrast, some compacts and collaborative ventures engage in political action to bring about *reform* in school policy and practice. School improvement is too modest a goal for troubled districts that will require deep structural changes in teaching, learning, and educational decision making, restructuring educational governance through school-site councils, decentralization, choice, and other plans. In these communities, business leaders are willing to commit extra resources and moral support to their local districts, but only for the quid pro quo of change and improvement. They set their own expectations and agendas for school reform. The Boston Compact is the most prominent and fascinating example. Begun ten years ago, the Compact promised extra resources to the school district but at the same time established clear goals for school improvement as part of the deal. In the formal agreement signed by the business community and the school district in 1982, business guaranteed high school graduates jobs and college aid in return for systemwide improvements in student performance, particularly in Boston's high dropout rate.

But the Boston Compact discovered that the expectation of change and the reality of change are two different things. After six years, even though local firms exceeded hiring goals, only marginal gains had been made in the reading ability of graduates, and the dropout rate in the district had actually increased. Business leaders refused to renew the agreement with the Boston public schools until they received assurances that the pace of reform would pick up.

In the renegotiated Compact II, Boston's business leaders sought to establish clearer expectations for change, with specific consequences for business involvement and support. As a result, in January 1989, the Boston School Committee restructured the Boston public schools to allow for decentralized decision making and parental choice. The plan established "controlled choice" within the Boston public schools, technical assistance for schools unsuccessful in recruiting students, and school improvement and planning councils made up of parents, educators, and business and other community representatives. And in May 1989, the Boston Teachers Union and city school system reached tentative agreement on a new system of school-based management and accountability for Boston's schools.

These changes in both strategy and demand have led Boston's business community into a new era of involvement in education reform. According to one business leader involved in the Compact, "the first phase of our involvement was relatively easy and rewarding, but the magnitude of change that needs to occur to provide effective education for disadvantaged children and youth makes our job harder and harder." Business needs to have real staying power in the years ahead because "real education reform is not all peaches and cream."

Subsequently, the National Alliance of Business has used the Boston Compact's strategy for promoting educational reform in its efforts to organize business involvement in education in eleven other cities: Cincinnati, Detroit, Indianapolis, Louisville, Memphis, Miami/Dade County, Pittsburgh, Providence, Rochester, San Diego, and Seattle. It derived several principles from the experience of the Boston Compact:

- Develop long-term, measurable goals.
- Designate a business intermediary.
- Develop a planning structure.
- Establish baseline data.
- Secure financial resources.
- Organize collaboration.

This model establishes an alternative forum for setting district goals and evaluating district performance outside the realm of the school board and the district's central administration and enables compacts to take a firm stance on reform goals that are not met. The challenge for the compact in each of these cities will be to create effective pressure for districtwide improvement and reform.

The strategy and tactics of business leaders in Chicago were more radical and ambitious. Yet, convinced that the Chicago public schools were too disorganized and ineffective for conventional improvement strategies to succeed, business and community leaders demanded major structural reforms. Together, they lobbied the Illinois State Legislature to enact the nation's most dramatic effort to restructure urban education. In the Chicago school reform plan, school decision making and governance moved from the central office and city school board to individual schools and included parents, teachers, and administrators. Local school councils, made up of 3,500 parents elected by the community, have authority to adopt school improvement efforts, hire and fire principals, and allocate school budgets.

As was the case in Boston, the Chicago business community arrived at its current posture only after years of sustained involvement. At the beginning of the decade, Chicago United had organized a massive program of management assistance to the schools;

and by the mid-1980s, Chicago chief executives officers were participating in Mayor Washington's Summit on Education to identify school reform needs.

In 1987, though, the business community threw its support behind the growing voices of dissatisfaction among parent and community groups during the city's longest teachers' strike. By the following year, Chicago United and the business community's Leadership for Quality Education were (and have remained) dedicated to the radical legislative reforms, a far cry from the management assistance efforts of a decade ago.

Only a few compacts and collaborative efforts have ventured into the arena of political demands for school reform. There may be a surge in such efforts over the next few years as businesspeople gain greater experience in and knowledge of educational improvement, their local schools, and their own latent influence and as the need for school change, driven by demographic, social, and economic changes, becomes more urgent.

Is one strategy for reform better than another? Do any of the different relationships at the local level (helping-hand relationships, programmatic initiatives, compacts and collaborative ventures) make a difference? It is too soon to judge. Most school-business relationships are predicated on the assumption that business will support the changes and adjustments educators themselves believe are necessary. Mini-grants, for example, provide teachers and principals with the extra funds to carry out special projects in math, science, reading, writing, and other curriculum areas. They do not challenge the professional authority or expertise of teachers, but instead invite them to redesign different aspects of their programs.

Most compacts and collaborative efforts do not challenge districtwide practices either. Instead, they provide a coordinating mechanism for a variety of efforts to support changes and programmatic improvements identified by educators. To some, this strategy is too soft; to others, it is empowerment. However, the growing instances of more critical demands being placed on school systems suggest that simply supporting schools and school districts will not be sufficient; business leaders can help bring about changes in the system if they are willing to become knowledgeable, remain extensively involved, and take political risks.

POLICY CHANGE

The 1980s were a time of intensive education policy making in almost every state in the Union, producing new laws and regulations of unprecedented scope and number. The business community was quickly drawn into this activity, both by its own growing engagement in local educational affairs and by the strong invitation of state political leadership.

Thus, the origins and organization of business involvement at the state level differ greatly from the local experience. Contemporary business involvement at the state level began as political action, not as supportive services. Moreover, the alliances differ: Business leadership was brought in at the state level as part of a new coalition for education reform spearheaded by governors and legislators, more than educators.

This new coalition, dedicated to reform, often challenged existing policy as well as the traditional policy-making authority of state school boards, state school superintendents, and other traditional education interests. In fact, in many states, it amounted to an alternative system for educational policy making.

The differences between business involvement at the state and local levels stem in part from the different roles state and local governments play in our federal system. Educational policy making at the state level has usually sought to establish uniform (most often minimum) standards with attendant regulations, certification, and accreditation processes and funding formulas; at the local level, educational policy making has traditionally emphasized shaping schools to local priorities.

During the 1960s and 1970s, business was not a prominent participant in state educational politics. Education was considered a political backwater, under the control of a few traditional professional, legislative, and bureaucratic interests. During the 1970s, in fact, business involvement in many states was anything but supportive of public education, concentrating as it did on support of tax-limitation measures by referendum in California and Massachusetts and by law elsewhere.

Contemporary business involvement in state educational policy reform emerged when governors and state legislators began to engage corporate leaders in their new economic development and employment policy efforts. The fiscal condition of the states was extremely tenuous a decade ago; many states experienced their worst budget crises since the Great Depression. Intense international and interstate economic competitiveness for high-growth, high-technology industry made it increasingly clear that the nature of state policy making in economic development, employment, and education needed to change. Economic development no longer meant simply tax abatements to lure industry, for that strategy attracted businesses with little long-term commitment, which were easily lured away by more generous tax benefits or cost savings in other states and nations. Changes in federal employment policy through the Job Training Partnership Act mandated business participation in policy formation and program governance and provided a model for public and private cooperation in human resource policy making. More and more, investment in human capital and its cultivation became the focus of both economic development and employment policies.

It was inevitable that this economic development theme would extend to education reform in the states because state governments devote more resources to public education than to any other public service. It was also inevitable, given the new view of economic and human resource development emerging in the states, that business leaders would become prominently involved in efforts to reform education.

Substantively, the first wave of state reform activity concentrated on creating and raising standards for public schools and accountability for student achievement, teacher effectiveness, and administrative performance. These were congenial goals for business participants, reflecting their own operating style and (sometimes simplified) view of how organizations should perform. In pursuing this agenda, the governors and legislators, with business participation and support, were not hesitant to override the traditional policy-making responsibilities of state boards and superintendents. Between 1983 and 1985 alone, they created more than 300 special state task forces and commissions to reform education through new standards and procedures from the top down. Business played an important role. Its representatives constituted almost 25 percent of the membership of these task forces: 9 percent of the participants on task forces sponsored by educators but 31 percent on task forces sponsored by governors and state legislators. And in many key instances, a business leader was designated to head the task force.

Once standards and accountability schemes were established, business involvement in state educational policy took the new form of representation on newly mandated special councils that oversee the implementation of reform, superseding in whole or in part the responsibilities of state boards and agencies.

Business leaders have participated in state policy developments in different ways. In the vast majority of cases, business became involved in policy making by invitation rather than by initiating reform itself. In response to gubernatorial and legislative calls to action, business leaders participated in special task forces and commissions to set educational agendas, lobbied for special causes, gave testimony before state legislatures, and *mirabile dictu,* supported tax increases to pay for the new reforms. Such involvement was particularly notable in the mid-1980s in Mississippi, Florida, South Carolina, and throughout the South, where the most remarkable changes in policies and budgets took place. Later in the decade, as state economic conditions worsened, such instances of willingness to consider new taxes became rare and business support for education funding was far less secure.

Less frequently, though most visibly, the business community furnished the principal impetus for state education reforms. Business Roundtables in California, Washington, and Minnesota and Ross Perot in Texas established their own agendas and coalitions for reform early in the decade. More recently, business leaders and councils in Arkansas and Texas have tried to be similarly out in front, with varying persistence and effect. Very few of these out-front efforts have been successfully sustained. In California, for instance, the Business Roundtable's ambitious agendas for higher standards and accountability and expanded programs for teacher and school improvement were swiftly enacted along with new education funding in the early 1980s; but since then, the state's business community has not sustained a leadership role in the development of educational policy.

South Carolina has been exemplary in strategically guiding education reform through careful policy development and institutionalization. From the beginning, business leaders played an important role in South Carolina's education reforms. Since 1984, they have served on the state's Business-Education Subcommittee, created by the state's Educational Improvement Act of 1983 (EIA 1). The powers of the subcommittee were extended by the state's second education reform package, the Educational Improvement Act of 1989 (EIA 2), to include broad advisory powers and authorization to review proposed rules for all programs created by the reform legislation and to recommend candidates to head the newly created Office of Public Accountability in the education department. In short, it has a mandate to monitor continuously the progress of education reform.

So far, South Carolina's strategy for reform has paid off. The state has greatly expanded its support (up 33 percent in the first year of reform alone). Subsequently, the state has experienced some significant gains in the classroom: higher standardized test scores, increased attendance rates, and more positive public opinion about the schools. South Carolina is, in fact, a leading instance of business involvement in the second wave of reform, moving beyond standards and accountability to restructuring schools and otherwise enhancing the capacity of teachers to perform effectively.

Its most recent reform provides for:

- Incentives to encourage school-site restructuring
- Mandatory school-based programs for four-year-old at-risk children
- Grants for school-based education of parents with preschoolers
- Expanded compensatory education programs to bring students up to grade level
- Demonstration grants for model and pilot projects designed to reduce school dropout rates
- Encouragement for districts to develop curricula and evaluation procedures for teaching higher-order skills
- Expanded school accountability

In South Carolina, business support was crucial in launching education reform efforts, and this support has become increasingly significant over the years. As one advisor noted, "Business involvement in state educational policy issues has become more important in South Carolina because education has become more important to business."

In other states, where the reforms are either more recent or less ambitious, the patterns of business involvement in implementation efforts have not yet clearly evolved.

What have been the outcomes of the state education reforms business has fought so hard to obtain? Standards have indeed changed. Between 1980 to 1989, math requirements were raised in thirty-five states, science requirements in twenty-seven, social studies in twenty-one, and English and language arts in fourteen. Graduation requirements were raised in forty-three states.

Higher standards for entry into teacher preparation and teaching have been established in virtually every state (though some have continued or expanded loopholes that let unqualified persons teach).

State financial support for education increased about 20 percent in real terms between 1983 and 1987 (making states the source of more than half of the dollars given to public schools), and teachers' salaries rose just as markedly.

Nine states – Arkansas, Georgia, Kentucky, New Jersey, New Mexico, Ohio, South Carolina, Texas, and West Virginia – passed academic bankruptcy laws allowing them to seize and operate the state's worst schools.

Has state policy activity improved student learning and performance? Judgments here are mixed. The National Assessment of Educational Progress shows small gains for minority students in several areas but insignificant and insufficient improvement across the board. Scholastic Aptitude Test scores likewise remain relatively unchanged, and U.S. students continue to perform near or below students in other developed nations. By many of the measures that were used to motivate the reform movement, significant gains in performance have not yet occurred.

But changes have been detected as a result of the state education reform movement. The Educational Testing Service estimates that the number of students studying geometry increased by 15 percent and the number studying chemistry and biology by 5 percent each in the past few years. The high school graduation rate rose slightly (1.6 percent) between 1982 and 1987 to 71.1 percent of the age cohort, and we have discovered that almost half of the students who drop out return to complete their education within a few years. Of the 17 percent of high school sophomores who dropped out of school in 1980, 46 percent had finished high school by 1984.

Finally, both the number and the measured aptitudes of new teacher candidates have risen in recent years (though neither is yet sufficient to our needs).

What specific impact has business had on state education reform initiatives? First and foremost, business has helped change the politics of educational policy making in the states. By becoming part of a new coalition, business leaders helped create a new era of educational decision making.

In many (if not most) states, the new reforms would not have passed without business support. Sometimes business is credited with creating a positive climate for education reform; in other cases, business has garnered the political support necessary to pass specific proposals in state legislatures, especially bills related to funding. In either case, it has frequently had enormous political influence. Many business and government leaders endorse the views of one business executive prominently involved in his state's education reform:

> *The legislature really listens to the business community. Three business calls to a legislator seem like a groundswell....They have been critical in stimulating the reform movement in this state.*

Businesspeople recognize the important role they have played in drawing attention to the crisis in public education and forcing action. But in some cases, business groups have taken contradictory stands on important education reform issues, leaving politicians few clues about which viewpoint represents business interests. In some states where business support for education reform is poorly organized, educators and politicians have little faith that any single business representative can really speak for the business community:

Business is very fragmented...small, large, commercial, technical, service.... Too often we make the assumption that one sector can speak for all of the others when this isn't the case. One person speaking for the "business community" is not possible.

But wherever business leaders have been well organized, took the time to learn about the issues, and stayed involved, they discovered that their viewpoint carried great weight and that lawmakers were eager to listen to and act on what they had to say.

The most recent and remarkable business-related developments in education policy making have occurred on the national scene. As the President and governors have met in an education summit and struggled to produce national goals and objectives, they have been cheered on by an impressive array of the nation's leading business organizations – the National Alliance of Business, the Committee for Economic Development, the Business Roundtable, the U.S. Chamber of Commerce, the National Association of Manufacturers, the Conference Board, the American Business Conference, and the U.S. Hispanic Chamber of Commerce – joined together in a Business Coalition for Education Reform. The NAB and the Business Roundtable have together produced a new blueprint and primer for continuing corporate involvement in education reform through projects, programs, and policies. And the agenda of the President and governors strongly reflects the business agenda for higher standards, accountability for outcomes, restructured schools, and greater concentration on early intervention for at-risk children and youths.

BUSINESS INVOLVEMENT AND IMPACT ON EARLY INTERVENTION AND PREVENTION STRATEGIES

The most recent and daring of the business community's interventions has been the promotion of early intervention and prevention strategies for at-risk children. Unfortunately, the impact and payoff of this initiative have not been nearly as systematic and far-reaching as those of the earlier efforts focused more directly on schools. In its 1987 report *Children in Need*, CED argued that early and sustained intervention in the lives of at-risk children and youths should be one of the nation's highest priorities. This was the first declaration about early intervention from the business community and among the first in the nation. Because it came from the business community rather than from child advocates, the report was influential in the programmatic and political development of proposals for children at risk in early childhood.

Since the report's release, several national- and state-level commissions, task forces, and forums have been established with business support and participation to address the needs of children living in poverty, child care and early education initiatives, improved health care for expectant mothers and their young children, and employer-sponsored benefits for parents and children. The federal government has expanded funding for Head Start (which now serves fewer than one in five eligible children) and in 1990 adopted ambitious new child care legislation. Many states and localities have developed innovative model programs in child development and child care. CED has often been called on to help advocate and shape such proposals in order to emphasize the business interest in early intervention and prevention strategies for at-risk children and youths.

Beyond the circle of executives engaged in these national activities, business leaders seem to have a markedly different attitude toward child development programs than toward educational reform. A handful of prominent spokesmen are convinced of the need for early intervention and prevention strategies, but most business leaders have not yet become actively involved. The problem is not lack of information. Business leaders seem to be quite familiar with the payoffs that early intervention and prevention strategies will provide. Instead, the problem seems to be one of ambivalence about taking action and uncertainty about the role business can or should play in child development issues.

Many government leaders, as well as the public at large, express a similar ambivalence toward government-sponsored early intervention and prevention efforts. Concerns about cost, about which institutions and agencies should deliver what kinds of services, and about government intrusion into the privacy of families contribute to this uncertainty. Thus, even though important instances of innovation can be found in some localities, the number of needy and eligible children unserved far outnumbers those served, and there is no pattern of public commitment or business involvement similar to the patterns that have emerged on behalf of educational reforms.

There is no disagreement about the growing severity of the problem: 12.6 million children under 18 are poor. They account for 39.5 percent of the nation's poor (replacing the elderly during the decade as the largest segment of poor).

Increases in the cost of living and housing, decreases in real earnings for many segments of the labor force, and a decline in the value of federal subsidies, welfare, and housing have worsened the conditions of poor families. A recent Census Bureau study comparing twelve developed nations found that the United States has the highest rate of teen pregnancies, the highest murder rate for young males, the second-highest infant mortality rate, the highest percentage of children with divorced parents, and along with Australia, the highest percentage of children in poverty. Among industrialized nations, only two do not provide universal health coverage and parental leave for children and parents: South Africa and the United States. Needless to say, for minority children, every one of these indicators paints an even more bleak picture of devastation and decline.

Measured against this outlook, public and private national initiatives during the 1980s were paltry at every level. There were few business efforts like Success by Six in Minneapolis, which sought to coordinate services, educate parents, and influence policy in the early childhood years. There were few instances like the Washington Business Roundtable's efforts to secure, through legislation, needed social, health, nutritional, and educational services for all at-risk preschool children or like the Governor's Day Care Conference in Massachusetts. There were few states like South Carolina, which with business support mandated school district services for at-risk four-year-olds. There were few cases of industries or firms greatly expanding services and support to their own employees who are parents of young children.

The ambivalence and caution of the business community in promoting early childhood programs had several sources:

- The perception of enormous additional costs, in contrast with the marginal additional expense of many education reforms

- The astounding confusion and complexity in the organization of early childhood and child care services, coupled with the absence of a single institution, such as the public schools, where such services can be provided

- Continuing uncertainty about the nature of business responsibilities, even for employees and their families

- Related reservations about the extent of public responsibility or intrusion in family matters

- The daunting prospect of hostile or indifferent legislators and policy makers

Many business leaders perceive a need for more political leadership on early childhood issues, especially at the federal level. "Business should influence the federal government to come out of the trees on these issues," said one, echoing the sentiments of many.

CHAPTER 3

INTERIM RESULTS

At the end of a decade of renewed corporate interest in education and child development, it is difficult to make generalizations about its nature or impact. Indeed, the varied and complex character of events and of the business community have become evident. Different parts of the business sector have entered the picture at different times in different places and at different levels of government, and there are significant parts of the business sector that have not participated at all. The manner of participation has varied, too, ranging from hostile or disinterested inaction, to shallow contacts, to profound involvement combining a good measure of social responsibility with an essential self-interest. The actual policies promoted and projects launched have varied greatly, too. The tendency has been toward more well-informed, appropriate, and effective action at the higher levels of both corporate management and public policy. There seem to be few second thoughts among business leaders who have been involved in the educational reform movement about the continuing importance and necessity of their efforts – sober assessments, yes; second thoughts, no.

Looking over the range of initiatives spawned in the last decade, the business sector should take pride and satisfaction in its work but, at the same time, recognize that its participation has not yet been fully adequate to the task.

- There are many thousands of new business-sponsored projects in up to half of the nation's schools, with notable concentrations in areas of urban poverty. Some involve only modest donations of time and equipment, but growing numbers are programmatic and political partnerships of considerable duration. The limitations of the initial efforts have become increasingly clear; they are unlikely to affect educational achievement directly or to solve the problems of policy, resources, and management that all school systems face. At the same time, they have had no adverse side effects. They have introduced many thousands of managers and employees to the realities of our public schools and motivated them to become involved in further partnerships with the schools. The more extensive and programmatic partnerships in a few communities have shown some gains in student outcomes. The communitywide councils and compacts that today characterize business support in the large cities have stimulated far-reaching policy changes in Boston, Chicago, and other cities.

- Almost every state has raised its requirements, standards, and accountability measures for teachers and students at the urging and with the assistance of business leadership. It is unlikely that the additional resources needed for these policy initiatives would have been available had the business community not been involved in the process. In state after state, political leaders give credit to business support for making the difference between success and failure in this first stage of educational reform.

- At the same time, it has become obvious that reform from the top down is not sufficient. This approach can do no more than set the stage for improved performance, school by school, classroom by classroom, and child by child. Thus, the more recent emphasis on policies that will strengthen the teaching profession and promote the restructuring of schools – a shift for which CED can take special credit – represents a new strategy, a second stage in reform. Here, the results of business intervention are less clear. The calls for professionalization and restructuring are far more recent. They align business closely with reformers who think fundamental and painful changes must be introduced to improve schools. Such proposals are controversial and threatening to many educators in both classrooms and administrative offices. Many fine educators are committed to existing roles and procedures that they seek to strengthen and improve but not to replace.

- Not surprisingly, there is also some business support for some version of "choice" policies that would create markets and rewards for educational effectiveness rather than relying on an unlikely restructuring of public bureaucracy. At the same time, business leaders with firsthand experience in education recognize the limits of school choice and fear that it will be viewed as a panacea.

- At the moment, neither restructuring nor choice policies command overwhelming business support; nor are they expanding quickly beyond the well-known experiments in a few states and large districts. The experience of Miami/Dade County, where a mild form of restructuring has produced measurable educational improvements in a number of schools, is so far rare. It will be several years before restructuring or choice plans are widespread, let alone proven effective.

- At the federal or national level, there is, for the first time in a decade, the opportunity for positive policy making in education and child development. The process has scarcely begun, but already the potential for a constructive business influence is evident. The auspicious collaboration between the President and the governors builds on the emerging business agenda with remarkable fidelity. The quest for national goals carries forward an emphasis on outcomes while acknowledging the diversity of appropriate standards and measures in states and localities and promotes the nation's continuing focus and consensual attack on the issues. The call for loosening federal program requirements is clearly tied to restructuring efforts. And the pleas for immediate expansion of federal early childhood programs such as Head Start give a clear priority to the problems of poverty and disadvantage and the strategy of early intervention. Moreover, the influence of the business community through the Business Roundtable and the Business Coalition for Education Reform in persuading the President to consider, first, any substantive agenda for federal action and, second, this particular agenda, has been manifest.

- Business's access to and involvement in the policy councils of education seems assured. Business-education compacts and collaboratives are active in most urban communities. The processes of state policy making in education have changed substantially with business participation and approval. A number of states – South Carolina, Ohio, Florida, Indiana, Maryland, Minnesota, and New Jersey, for example – have institutionalized a business role in state educational policy making by creating state-level business advisory councils and have officially encouraged the creation of school-business partnerships at the local level. Business is clearly part of the reform coalition at every level.

- This is not to say that business and education are fully comfortable together. Considerable suspicion and misunderstanding persist on both sides of the relationship, although they are gradually diminishing. Moreover, the nature of business's reservations is changing; concerns about education's motivation and capacity persist but are being replaced gradually by laments about timidity and lack of trust. As they become more knowledgeable about education and child development, business leaders are becoming more concerned that children's learning must take precedence over institutional defensiveness. Many are ready to support educators who want to redesign their field and, closer to home, their schools. In interview after interview, we found that this was the most common message business leaders wanted to send to educators.

- Educators' initial concerns are receding as well. There were and are legitimate fears that business does not understand educational problems and has unrealistic expectations and that business representatives will shy away from controversy and difficult commitments or, worse, seek advantages for individual firms or industries. Gradually, though, most educators are coming to understand that business does not wish to take over the schools or to use them for narrow promotional or vocational purposes and that business interest and support provide a welcome, indeed indispensable, boost to their efforts to gather political and financial support. Many applaud the business interest in their states and cities and have begun to take advantage of the opportunity that a new coalition for the schools provides. The prospect is for a continued development of shared interests and, ultimately, a strengthening of mutual understanding.

- There is a small but impressive research effort under way that is steadily refining our understanding of many of the difficult underlying policies and practices in the economy and in schools. CED's reports and the recent NAB report, *Blueprint for Business in Restructuring Education,* are themselves impressive analyses. But many questions remain. How specifically does technological or market change affect the knowledge and skill requirements of jobs? How do workers secure additional education, and what are its benefits to them and to their firms? How and where do people learn job skills? What kinds of education and training are effective in imparting such skills? How can such requirements be successfully amalgamated with broader academic objectives in curriculum and pedagogy? How can the distinctive educational needs of poverty's children best be served? Researchers are seeking answers to these questions, spurred on and supported by business interest; but this necessarily extended inquiry has only just begun and only on a small scale.

WHAT'S MISSING FROM THIS PICTURE?

The disappointing fact, though wholly predictable at this stage of business involvement, is that with only modest exceptions, there has been no widespread impact of business involvement on educational outcomes – on the number of children staying in school and doing better in their studies. The serious problems of our schools did not develop overnight. They have always been with us in some form, and their present aggravated character has been building for at least three decades. Moreover, these have been years in which the economy's changing demands, immigration, and expanding proportions of poor children have combined to make the task of school improvement more challenging. Substantial impact on educational performance at this stage would be surprising indeed. The reforms and improvements sought by business have only begun to reach the schools and change the educational programs of individual students. New state requirements that increase the amount of English, math, and science needed to graduate, for example, have said nothing about the content of the curriculum or the nature of students' learning experiences in these subjects. Exploration of the crucial link between contemporary workplace requirements and curricula has barely begun, with business taking significant initiative only in the area of technology.

And there are other shortcomings to be acknowledged. Business has paid little attention to continuing issues of desegregation and integration, and neither business nor education has been able to help the poorest, most vulnerable children succeed. Setting standards, accountability, restructuring, and professionalization do not address the immediate needs of these children; at best, they only set the stage for future success. Programmatic initiatives have not reached these most threatened children. Indeed, the implication of *Children in Need* is that only earlier, better, and broader efforts can give them a good chance in school and in life, and the results of such efforts may not be clearly visible for a generation.

ANOTHER KIND OF IMPACT: ON BUSINESS ITSELF

When considering the readiness of business to continue working with good effect on issues of education and child development, we should also assess the long-term organizational capacity it has created within and for itself.

In terms of basic awareness, business has surely made great progress. Today, human resource development is commonly named the most significant issue for the future of most industries, problems with raw materials, markets, taxes, takeovers, and debt notwithstanding. The demographic, technological, and economic trends leading to this focus on human capital seem irreversible; human development is coming to be regarded as the only long-term solution to many pressing economic problems. It is unlikely that corporate interest in education and child development will slacken soon.

Understanding of education's prospects and problems is likewise growing in the business community, as is its level of comfort with its significant but limited role in the broad coalition seeking reform and improvement in education and child development. Corporate philanthropy and contribution programs have in many cases been redirected to support for public school endeavors. We are beginning to see instances of policy changes in business permitting or encouraging employees to function more easily as parents, advisors, or trustees for schools and as caregivers or mentors for children.

There are, nonetheless, important concerns in the areas of leadership and institutionalization. The number of CEOs furnishing active leadership rose swiftly in the mid-1980s, but it has probably diminished since then. The veterans worry aloud that their younger counterparts or successors do not wholly share their concern or commitment.

The paucity of interested and active executives is more worrisome when we consider the rarity with which even the most committed have institutionalized educational concerns in corporate executive offices. Most often, existing staff officers – in public affairs, community relations, contributions, or personnel offices – have been given additional status, resources, and (sometimes) staff to advise the CEO and represent the corporation. But these marginal efforts have not always survived changes in management or in profit margins. Corporate giving is sometimes vulnerable to new mergers and acquisitions; two giving programs may be collapsed into one much smaller effort, or distant leadership and interest may replace the long-time focus of local managements. Worst of all, corporate giving is sometimes tinged with an inappropriate public relations emphasis.

In organizations of the business community at large, efforts to help companies build organizational capacity have just begun with the blueprints and primer put out by the NAB and Business Roundtable in 1990. Such institutionalization will be a necessary ingredient if the initiatives launched in the 1980s are to be realized in programs and progress in the 1990s.

THE EXEMPLARY EDUCATION-MINDED
BUSINESS EXECUTIVE

What do business leaders who succeed in educational arenas know and do? No one model for effective performance exists, but there is a pattern. Exemplary corporate leaders

- See the improvement of education and child development as matters of national survival.

- See their involvement in education as a matter of corporate survival more than social responsibility or community public relations.

- Approach their dealings with education with a sense of "controlled impatience."

- Are sensitive to the challenges and limitations schools face.

- Are critical of bloated education bureaucracies, institutional rigidities, timid leadership, and lack of trust (criticisms they have leveled at their own enterprises), but not of the expertise, intentions, or intellectual capacity of educators.

- Have come to understand the difficult and time-consuming nature of school system changes and the need to support and stick with a few good ideas for a long time.

- Do not believe there is a "silver bullet" or owner's manual to bring about educational improvement.

- Are convinced that the enthusiasm of teachers and students is the indispensable element in good schools.

- Appreciate the history and current reality of imperfect school-business relationships and their share of the responsibility:
  - The sometimes uneven and unreliable character of business involvement and commitment
  - The inveterate short-term perspective on change and results
  - The inevitably mixed motives in policy trade-offs between support for adequate education spending and reluctance to embrace new taxes

- Assure that their corporate activities are all of high quality, that local projects are well designed and supported but are not expected to replace or turn around the regular education program.

- Take clear and reasoned stands on important public issues in education and child development. Their voice can be counted on even though their support cannot always be presumed.

- Show up (which is 90 percent of success in life, as Woody Allen says), knowing that recurrent meetings and rituals are just as important as dramatic announcements and exciting political victories.

CHAPTER 4

THE NEEDS OF THE 1990s

As the 1990s begin, business has not completed its work or fully attained its objectives in any phase of its efforts to stimulate the reform and improvement of education. Progress has been made on every front, in some cases substantial progress, but there is clearly more to be done. What should be the emphases of business involvement in the coming decade?

1. **Stay the Course.** Trite though it is, this is the first piece of advice businesspeople give one another nowadays. It has taken a decade for business communities – local, state, and national – to arrive at a stable, comprehensive view of the problems they and education face and the roles they can play in improving the schools. The *investment* analysis, *restructuring* theme, and *at-risk* focus are clear-cut, powerful ideas that should guide business leadership in education for many years. They can have continuing impact in shaping local projects as well as policy development at every level of government.

2. **Promote National Dialogue and Federal Involvement.** President Bush should be helped in his intention to be an "education president." He is the first President to harbor such an ambition since Lyndon Johnson, whose administration built Head Start, Chapter I, and student aid, among other educational achievements. Many of the business leaders we spoke with were disappointed with the federal role during the last decade and made it clear that they do not see business involvement as a substitute for federal initiative.

The Education Summit of the President and the governors, held at the strong urging and with the support of business leadership, produced an agenda for national action that is wholly consistent with the points that business has been emphasizing: (a) a national goals program to guide and assist state and local efforts in educational improvement and to identify national political leadership with the effort for the long haul, (b) the use of existing federal programs and resources to facilitate and strengthen efforts at local reform and restructuring, and (c) expansion of federal programs such as Head Start to help more poor young people. Moreover, as the prospect of a peace dividend has been glimpsed (however dimly), education and child development, along with deficit reduction, are at the top of most lists of uses for it. Were the business leaders to promote these views with a clear and strong voice, they could be at the federal level in the 1990s what they often were at the state level in the 1980s: the political difference between success and failure.

3. **Pursue Related Human Service Perspectives.** *Children in Need* promotes the emerging perspective that no one agency or institution can effectively meet the multiple needs of the children of chronic and persistent poverty. By the time they reach school, for example, these children have often lacked health care (before, during, and after birth), encouragement and support from family and community, and child development services; and most of all, their families have lacked *income*. The business community has grown comfortable in working with the schools but is less enthusiastic about working with other human service agencies. In the 1990s, business should create in related human service fields the comprehensive analyses and action programs that they developed and executed with respect to education during the 1980s. Above all, they must continue to explore and correct the ways in which poverty, discrimination, or indifference undermine the lives of many children and make more difficult the tasks of the institutions serving them.

4. **Build the Infrastructure of Business-Education Partnerships.** Except at the federal level, dramatic education policy interventions inspired by business leadership will probably be rare in the 1990s. The tasks of these years will be less visible:

   –Preserving political, programmatic, and financial gains in less glamorous times

   –Supporting the local implementation of reforms such as school restructuring

   –Participating in the slow work of reshaping and strengthening curricula

   –Building deeper understanding between businessmen and educators on the path from skepticism through acceptance to trust

   – Strengthening the capacity of business representatives to participate in educational improvement through organizational and professional development

These steps will redeem the promise of the 1980s.

5. **Support Pertinent Research and Analysis.** The activity of the 1980s has not been solely rhetoric, organization, and action. There has been considerable progress in our understanding of the factors underlying economic and technological changes, human learning, and effective educational practice. Business has a direct interest in new discoveries in these areas for its own activities but also for its understanding of educational institutions. It has given such research little support or priority in its own sphere or in its recommendations for public policy.

6. **Review and Assess Business's Own Commitment and Performance.** This report may be the beginning of such assessments, but no more than that. There is a paucity of evaluative research in the field and few plans to accomplish it.

Business must learn how to hold *itself* accountable in this field. There are, for example, several recommendations in *Investing in Our Children* that are directed primarily to operations of the business community itself: encouraging and facilitating employees' participation in local educational activities, developing systems for regular feedback to the schools, stimulating the redesign of vocational education programs and expanding cooperative education opportunities, making management training and assistance available to the schools, and becoming involved in the creation of intermediary institutions such as partnerships and local education foundations. Our knowledge of progress in these areas is sketchy.

Also, business leadership must continue to deepen its understanding of our nation's education enterprise and its role therein. Agendas will change. Frustrations will grow. Differences in views may well increase, both within the business community and between it and educators, concerning the efficiency and effectiveness of schools, as well as the need for and shape of new resources and programs of improvement. Only continuing reflection and analysis will produce an influential and appropriate business perspective on education's ever-present problems.

CONCLUSION

Education in the 1980s was the scene of a great deal of energetic leadership from within the field and from without. A profusion of good ideas for reform and improvement have been derived from new research, the experience of other fields (including business), and plain common sense. By contrast with the beginning of the decade, the situation today should not engender despair; rather, it should stimulate hope and determination to succeed. It will take all of the 1990s to redeem the promise of the 1980s. With "controlled impatience," business must remain in the midst of the enterprise.

BIBLIOGRAPHY

EDUCATION REFORM: THE GREAT DEBATE

Adler, Mortimer J. *The Paideia Proposal: An Educational Manifesto.* New York: Macmillan Publishing, 1982.

American Association for the Advancement of Science. *Education in the Sciences: A Developing Crisis.* Washington, D.C.: American Association for the Advancement of Science, April 1982.

Anderson, Richard C., Elfrieda H. Hiebert, Judith A. Scott, Ian A. G. Wilkinson, and the Commission on Reading. *Becoming a Nation of Readers: The Report of the Commission on Reading.* Washington, D.C.: National Institute of Education, 1984.

Bennet, William J. *American Education: Making It Work.* A Report to the President and the American People. Washington, D.C.: U.S. Department of Education, April 1988.

————. *First Lessons: A Report on Elementary Education in America.* Washington, D.C.: U.S. Department of Education, September 1986.

Bloom, Allan. *The Closing of the American Mind.* New York: Simon and Schuster, 1987.

Boyer, Ernest L. *College: The Undergraduate Experience in America.* New York: Harper and Row, 1987.

————. *High School: A Report on Secondary Education in America.* New York: Harper and Row, 1983.

Carnegie Council on Adolescent Development. *Turning Points: Preparing American Youth for the 21st Century.* New York: Carnegie Corporation, June 1989.

Carnegie Forum on Education and the Economy. *A Nation Prepared: Teachers for the 21st Century.* A Report of the Task Force on Teaching as a Profession. New York: Carnegie Forum on Education and the Economy, 1986.

Carnegie Foundation for the Advancement of Teaching. *An Imperiled Generation: Saving Urban Schools.* Princeton, N.J.: Princeton University Press, 1988.

————. *Report Card on School Reform: The Teachers Speak.* Princeton, N.J.: Carnegie Foundation for the Advancement of Teaching, 1988.

Cheney, Lynne V. *American Memory: A Report on the Humanities in the Nation's Public Schools.* Washington, D.C.: National Endowment for the Humanities, 1986.

Children's Defense Fund. *Children 1990: A Report Card, Briefing Book, and Action Primer.* Washington, D.C.: Children's Defense Fund, January 1990.

Clifford, Geraldine Jonsich, and James W. Guthrie. *Ed School: A Brief for Professional Education.* Chicago: University of Chicago Press, 1988.

Cohen, Michael. *Restructuring the Education System: Agenda for the '90s.* Washington, D.C.: National Governors' Association, 1989.

Coleman, James S., Thomas Hoffer, and Sally Kilgore. *High School Achievement: Public, Catholic, and Private Schools Compared.* New York: Basic Books, 1982.

College Entrance Examination Board. *Academic Preparation for College: What Students Need to Know and Be Able to Do.* New York: College Entrance Examination Board, 1983.

———. *Academic Preparation in the Arts.* New York: College Entrance Examination Board, 1985.

———. *Academic Preparation in English.* New York: College Entrance Examination Board, 1985.

———. *Academic Preparation in Mathematics.* New York: College Entrance Examination Board, 1985.

———. *Equality and Excellence: The Educational Status of Black Americans.* New York: College Entrance Examination Board, 1985.

Committee on Policy for Racial Justice. *Visions of a Better Way: A Black Appraisal of Public Schooling.* Washington, D.C.: Joint Center for Political Studies Press, 1989.

Dealing with Dropouts: The Urban Superintendents' Call to Action. Washington, D.C.: U.S. Department of Education, Office of Educational Research and Improvement, November 1987.

Education Commission of the States. *A Summary of Major Reports on Education.* Denver, Colo.: Education Commission of the States, 1983.

———. *Action for Excellence: A Comprehensive Plan to Improve Our Nation's Schools.* Denver, Colo.: Education Commission of the States, 1983.

———. *Action in the States.* Denver, Colo.: Education Commission of the States, July 1984.

Finn, Chester E., Jr., Diane Ravitch, and Robert T. Fancher. *Against Mediocrity: The Humanities in America's High Schools.* New York: Holmes and Meier Publishers, 1984.

———, and P. Holley Roberts. *Challenges to the Humanities.* New York: Holmes and Meier Publishers, 1985.

Ford Foundation. *The Common Good: Social Welfare and the American Future: Policy Recommendations of the Executive Panel.* New York: Ford Foundation, May 1989.

The Forgotten Half: Pathways to Success for America's Youth and Young Families. Washington, D.C.: William T. Grant Foundation Commission on Work, Family and Citizenship, November 1988.

The Forgotten Half: Non-College Youth in America. Interim Report on the School-to-Work Transition. Washington, D.C.: William T. Grant Foundation Commission on Work, Family and Citizenship, January 1988.

Gifford, Bernard R., ed., *History in the Schools: What Shall We Teach?* New York: Macmillan Publishing, 1988.

Goodlad, John I. *A Place Called School.* New York: McGraw-Hill, 1984.

————, and Pamela Keating, eds. *Access to Knowledge: An Agenda for Our Nation's Schools.* New York: College Entrance Examination Board, 1990.

Grubb, W. Norton, and Marvin Lazerson. *Broken Promises: How Americans Fail Their Children.* New York: Basic Books, 1982.

Hahn, Andrew, Jacqueline Danzberger, and Bernard Lefkowitz. *Dropouts in America: Enough Is Known for Action.* Washington, D.C.: Institute for Educational Leadership, March 1987.

Harris, Louis, and associates. *Redesigning America's Schools: The Public Speaks.* Survey for the Carnegie Forum on Education and the Economy. New York: Carnegie Corporation, 1986.

Holmes Group Executive Board. *Tomorrow's Teachers: A Report of the Holmes Group.* East Lansing, Mich.: Homes Group Executive Board, 1986.

Jacobson, Willard J., Rodney L. Doran, Edith T. Chang, Eve Humrich, and John P. Keeves. *The Second IEA Science Study–U.S.* New York: Teachers College International Association for the Evaluation of Educational Achievement, 1987.

Levin, Henry M. "The Educationally Disadvantaged: A National Crisis." State Youth Initiatives Project, Working Paper no. 6. Philadelphia: Public/Private Ventures, 1985.

National Center on Education and the Economy. *To Secure Our Future: The Federal Role in Education.* Rochester, N.Y.: National Center on Education and the Economy, 1989.

National Center for Improving Science Education. *Getting Started in Science: A Blueprint for Elementary School Science Education.* Andover, Mass. and Washington, D.C.: Network, Inc., 1989.

National Coalition of Advocates for Students. *Barriers to Excellence: Our Children at Risk.* Boston, Mass.: National Coalition of Advocates for Students, 1985.

National Commission for Excellence in Education. *A Nation at Risk: The Imperative for Educational Reform.* Washington, D.C.: U.S. Government Printing Office, 1983.

National Commission on Excellence in Educational Administration. *Leaders for America's Schools.* Bloomington, Ind.: University Council for Educational Administration, 1987.

National Commission on Social Studies in the Schools. *Charting a Course: Social Studies for the 21st Century.* Report of the Curriculum Task Force. Washington, D.C.: National Commission on Social Studies in the Schools, November 1989.

National Governors' Association. *The Governors' Report on Education: Results in Education.* Washington, D.C.: National Governors' Association. Separate reports issued in 1987, 1988, 1989, 1990.

————.*Time for Results: The Governors' 1991 Report on Education.* Washington, D.C.: National Governors' Association, 1986.

————.*The First Sixty Months.* Washington, D.C.: National Governors' Association, 1987.

National Policy Board for Educational Administration. *Improving the Preparation of School Administrators: An Agenda for Reform.* Charlottesville, Va.: National Policy Board for Educational Administration, University of Virginia, May 1989.

The Nation's Report Card: Improving the Assessment of Student Achievement. Report of the Study Group, Lamar Alexander, Chairman. Cambridge, Mass.: National Academy of Education, Harvard Graduate School of Education, 1987.

National Science Board Commission on Precollege Education in Mathematics, Science and Technology. *Educating Americans for the 21st Century.* Washington, D.C.: National Science Foundation, 1983.

Oxley, Diana. *Effective Dropout Prevention: The Case for Schoolwide Reform.* New York: Public Education Association, May 1988.

Public Schools of Choice. Alexandria, Va.: Association for Supervision and Curriculum Development, 1990.

Schorr, Lisabeth B., with Daniel Schorr. *Within Our Reach: Breaking the Cycle of Disadvantage.* New York: Doubleday, 1988.

Sizer, Theodore R. *Horace's Compromise: The Dilemma of the American High School.* Boston: Houghton Mifflin Company, 1984.

Twentieth Century Fund. *Making the Grade.* Report of the Twentieth Century Fund Task Force on Federal Elementary and Secondary Education Policy. New York: Twentieth Century Fund, 1983.

BUSINESS REPORTS AND ACTIVITIES

Asche, J. *Handbook for Principals and Teachers: A Collaborative Approach for the Effective Involvement of Community and Business Volunteers at the School Site.* Alexandria, Va.: National Association of Partners in Education, 1989.

Ashwell, A., and F. Caropreso. *Business Leadership: The Third Wave of Education Reform.* New York: The Conference Board, 1989.

Bednarek, David. *Chicago Business Leadership and School Reform.* Occasional Paper no. 3. Washington, D.C.: Institute for Educational Leadership and the Edna McConnell Clark Foundation, November 1989.

Berman, Paul, and associates. *Restructuring California Education: A Design for Public Education in the 21st Century.* Berkeley, Calif., 1988.

Blank, Martin. *Next Steps in the Relationship between Business and Public Schools.* Occasional Paper no. 1. Washington, D.C.: Institute for Educational Leadership and Edna McConnell Clark Foundation, February 1988.

Bowles, Samuel, and Herbert Gintis. *Schooling in Capitalist America: Educational Reform and the Contradictions of Economic Life.* New York: Basic Books, 1976.

Bowsher, Jack E. *Educating America: Lessons Learned in the Nation's Corporations.* New York: John Wiley and Sons, 1989.

Boyer, Ernest L. *School Reform: A National Strategy.* Washington, D.C.: Business Roundtable, 1989.

———. "Why Should the Private Sector Support Public Education?" *Foundation News* (November/December 1982): 4-11.

Business and the Public Schools. Special theme issue of *Peabody Journal of Education* 63, no. 2 (Winter 1986). Marsha Levine and Denis P. Doyle, eds.

Business-Higher Education Forum. *American Potential: The Human Dimension.* Washington, D.C.: Business-Higher Education Forum, 1988.

———. *America's Competitive Challenge: The Need for a National Response.* A Report to the President of the United States. Washington, D.C.: Business-Higher Education Forum, April 1983.

Business Response to Education in America. Study sponsored by *Fortune* and Allstate Insurance. New York: Time Inc. Magazine Company, 1989.

Business Roundtable. *The Role of Business in Education Reform: Blueprint for Action.* New York: Business Roundtable, 1988.

Callahan, Raymond E. *Education and the Cult of Efficiency.* Chicago: University of Chicago Press, 1962.

Carnoy, Martin, and Henry M. Levin. *Schooling and Work in the Democratic State.* Stanford, Calif.: Stanford University Press, 1985.

Center for Public Resources. *Basic Skills in the U.S. Work Force: The Contrasting Perceptions of Business, Labor, and Public Education.* New York: Center for Public Resources, February 1983.

Committee for Economic Development. *Business and the Schools.* A CED Symposium, Los Angeles, California. New York: Committee for Economic Development, September 1984.

———. *Children in Need: Investment Strategies for the Educationally Disadvantaged.* New York: Committee for Economic Development, 1987.

———. *Investing in America's Future.* New York: Committee for Economic Development, 1988.

———. *Investing in Our Children.* New York: Committee for Economic Development, 1985.

———. *CED and Education: National Impact and Next Steps.* A CED Symposium. New York: Committee for Economic Development, 1988.

———. *Work and Change: Labor Market Adjustment Policies in a Competitive World.* New York: Committee for Economic Development, 1987.

Council for Aid to Education. *Business and the Schools: A Guide to Effective Programs.* New York: Council for Aid to Education, 1989.

Council for Financial Aid to Education. *What American Corporations Are Doing to Improve the Quality of Precollege Education: A CFAE Sampler.* New York: Council for Financial Aid to Education, December 1985.

Cronin, Joseph M. *Business Assistance to Urban College-Bound Students: Models that Work.* Occasional Paper no. 4. Washington, D.C.: Institute for Educational Leadership and the Edna McConnell Clark Foundation, March 1989.

Cuban, Larry. "You're on the Right Track, David." *Phi Delta Kappan* 69, no. 8 (April 1988): 571-572.

Dayton, Charles, Alan Weisberg, and David Stern. *California Partnership Academies: 1987-88 Evaluation Report.* Policy Paper PP89-9-1. Berkeley, Calif.: Policy Analysis for California Education, September 1989.

Doyle, Denis P. "Endangered Species: Children of Promise." Special Advertising Section, *Business Week,* 1989.

Eurich, Nell P. *Corporate Classrooms: The Learning Business.* Lawrenceville, N.J.: Princeton University Press, 1985.

Farrar, Eleanor, and Anthony Cipollone. "After the Signing: The Boston Compact, 1982-1985." Paper commissioned by the Edna McConnell Clark Foundation, August 1985.

————. *The Business Community and School Reform: The Boston Compact at Five Years.* Buffalo, N.Y.: State University of New York at Buffalo, December 1987.

————, and Colleen Connolly. *Improving Middle Schools in Boston: A Report on Boston Compact and School District Initiatives.* Buffalo, N.Y.: State University of New York at Buffalo, September 1989.

Getting Down to Business: Next Steps in School Business Partnerships. Report on an Exploratory Conference, February 24, 1988. Occasional Paper no. 2. Washington, D.C.: Institute for Educational Leadership and the Edna McConnell Clark Foundation, May 1988.

Goldberg, Peter. *Corporate Advocacy for Public Education.* Occasional Paper no. 5. Washington, D.C.: Institute for Educational Leadership and Edna McConnell Clark Foundation, March 1989.

Kearns, David T. "An Education Recovery Plan for America." *Phi Delta Kappan* 69, no. 8 (April 1988): 565-570.

————."Education Recovery: Business Must Set the Agenda. An Open Letter to Our 41st President." Presented at the Economic Club of Detroit, Xerox Corporation, October 26, 1987.

————, and Denis P. Doyle. *Winning the Brain Race: A Bold Plan to Make Our Schools Competitive.* San Francisco, Calif.: Institute for Contemporary Studies, 1988.

Kirst, Michael W. "The California Business Roundtable: Their Strategy and Impact on State Education Policy." Paper prepared for the Committee for Economic Development, New York, 1983.

Kolderie, Ted. "Education that Works: The Right Role for Business." *Harvard Business Review* (September-October 1987): 56-62.

Labor Force 2000: Corporate America Responds. Allstate Forum on Public Issues. Northbrook, Ill., 1989.

Lacey, Richard A., and Christopher Kingsley. *A Guide to Working Partnerships.* Waltham, Mass.: Brandeis University Center for Human Resources, 1988.

Lazerson, Marvin, and W. Norton Grubb. *American Education and Vocationalism.* New York: Teachers College Press, 1974.

Levine, Marsha, and Roberta Trachtman, eds. *American Business and the Public School: Case Studies of Corporate Involvement in Public Education.* New York: Teachers College Press, 1988.

Lewis, Anne. *Getting Down to Business: Next Steps in School-Business Partnerships.* Occasional Paper no. 2. Washington, D.C.: Institute for Educational Leadership, May 1988.

Lund, Leonard. *Beyond Business/Education Partnerships: The Business Experience.* Research Report no. 918. New York: Conference Board, 1988.

Magnet, Myron. "How to Smarten Up the Schools." *Fortune,* 1 February 1988, pp. 86-94.

Mann, Dale. "All That Glitters: Public School/Private Sector Interaction in Twenty-Three U.S. Cities." A report prepared for the Exxon Education Foundation, New York, September 1984.

―――. *Business Involvement and Public School Improvement: A National Review of Local Evidence.* New York: Center for Education and the American Economy, November 20, 1986.

―――."The Honeymoon Is Over." *Phi Delta Kappan* 69, no. 8 (April 1988): 573-575.

McMullan, Bernard J., and Phyllis Snyder. *Allies in Education: Schools and Businesses Working Together for At-Risk Youth.* Volume 1, *Findings from the National Assessment.* Philadelphia: Public/Private Ventures, Fall 1987.

―――, et al. *Allies in Education: Schools and Businesses Working Together for At-Risk Youth.* Volume 2, *Collaboration Profiles.* Philadelphia : Public/ Private Ventures, Fall 1987.

Mecklenburger, James A. "Neither Schools nor Photocopiers Are Flawless." *Phi Delta Kappan* 69, no. 8 (April 1988): 574-575.

Minnesota Business Partnership Educational Quality (K-12) Task Force. *Educating Students for the 21st Century.* Minneapolis, Minn.: Minnesota Business Partnership, November 12, 1984.

National Alliance of Business. *A Blueprint for Business on Restructuring Education.* Washington, D.C.: National Alliance of Business, 1989.

―――."Business and Education: The Demand for Partnership."Special Advertising Section, *Business Week,* 2 May 1988.

―――. *The Compact Project: School-Business Partnerships for Improving Education.* Washington, D.C.: National Alliance of Business, 1989.

―――. *Shaping Tomorrow's Workforce.* Washington, D.C.: National Alliance of Business, 1988.

National Center for Education Statistics. *Education Partnerships in Public Elementary and Secondary Schools.* Survey Report CS 89-060. Washington, D.C.: U.S. Department of Education, Office of Educational Research and Improvement, February 1989.

Panel on Secondary School Education for the Changing Workplace. *High Schools and the Changing Workplace: The Employers' View.* Washington, D.C.: National Academy Press, 1984.

"Partnership: Building Links Between Schools and Communities." Special theme issue of *Phi Delta Kappan* 65, no. 6 (February 1984). David S. Seeley, ed.

Partnerships for Learning: School Completion and Employment Preparation in the High School Academies. New York: Academy for Educational Development, 1989.

Patrick, Cynthia L. *School-Industry "Partnership Academies": Programs that Work.* Occasional Paper no. 11. Washington, D.C.: Institute for Educational Leadership and Edna McConnell Clark Foundation, September 1989.

Perry, Nancy. "Saving the Schools: How Business Can Help." *Fortune,* 7 November 1988, pp. 42-46.

Peterson, Terry. *Sustained Business Involvement in State School Reform: The South Carolina Story.* Occasional Paper no. 11. Washington, D.C.: Institute for Educational Leadership and Edna McConnell Clark Foundation, August 1989.

Preparing Schools for the 1990s: An Essay Collection. New York: Metropolitan Life Insurance Company, 1989.

Reingold, Janet. *The Fourth R: Workforce Readiness. A Guide to Business Education Partnerships.* Washington, D.C.: National Alliance of Business, 1987.

Siegel, Peggy M., and Eugene R. Smoley, Jr. *Reaching Common Ground: Advancing Business Participation in Restructuring Education.* Occasional Paper no. 6. Washington, D.C.: Institute for Educational Leadership and Edna McConnell Clark Foundation, April 1989.

————. *Restructuring Education: Parallels with the Private Sector.* Washington, D.C.: National Governors' Association, March 1988.

Spring, Joel H. *Education and the Rise of the Corporate State.* Boston: Beacon Press, 1972.

Timpane, P. Michael. "Business Has Rediscovered the Public Schools." *Phi Delta Kappan* 65, no. 6 (February 1984): 389-392.

————. "Business Involvement in U.S. Education." *Canadian Business Review 17* (Autumn 1990): 17-20.

————. *Corporations and Public Education in the Cities.* Report supported by Carnegie Corporation. New York: Teachers College, Columbia University, May 1982.

Trimble, Grace. *Moving Beyond Fuzzy Altruism in Business-Education Relationships: The Potential of the Georgia Alliance for Public Education.* Washington, D.C.: Institute for Educational Leadership and Edna McConnell Clark Foundation, June 1989.

Union Carbide Task Force on Education. *Undereducated Uncompetitive USA.* Danbury, Conn.: Union Carbide Corporation, 1989.

United Way of America. *What Lies Ahead: Looking Toward the '90s.* Alexandria, Va.: United Way of America Strategic Planning Division, 1987.

U.S. Department of Labor. *Employers and Child Care: Benefiting Work and Family.* Washington, D.C.: U.S. Government Printing Office, 1989.

Woodside, William S. "Corporate Leadership for Public Education." Occasional Paper on Leadership Issues no. 1. Washington, D.C.: Institute for Educational Leadership, 1986.

———. "Education: A Public Role for the Private Sector." Remarks presented to the New York Teacher-Business Roundtable, St. Regis Hotel, January 14, 1986.

THE HISTORICAL AND POLITICAL CONTEXT FOR REFORM

Allen, Russell, Norman Bettis, Dana Kurfman, Walter MacDonald, Ina V.S. Mullis, and Christopher Salter. *The Geography Learning of High-School Seniors.* NAEP. Prepared by Educational Testing Service. Washington, D.C.: U.S. Department of Education, Office of Educational Research and Improvement, February 1990.

Applebee, Arthur N., Judith A. Langer, Lynn B. Jenkins, Ina V.S. Mullis, and Mary A. Foertsch. *Learning to Write in Our Nation's Schools: Instruction and Achievement in 1988 at Grades 4, 8, and 12.* NAEP. Prepared by the Educational Testing Service. Washington, D.C.: U.S. Department of Education, Office of Educational Research and Improvement, June 1990.

———, and Ina V.S. Mullis. *Crossroads in American Education: A Summary of Findings.* NAEP. Princeton, N.J.: Educational Testing Service, February 1989.

———. *Grammar, Punctuation, and Spelling: Controlling the Conventions of Written English at Ages 9, 13, and 17.* NAEP Report no. 15-W-03. Princeton, N.J.: Educational Testing Service, June 1987.

———. *Writing: Trends Across the Decade, 1974-84.* NAEP Report no. 15-W-01. Princeton, N.J.: Educational Testing Service, 1984.

———. *The Writing Report Card: Writing Achievement in American Schools.* NAEP Report no. 15-W-02. Princeton, N.J.: Educational Testing Service, November 1986.

———. *Who Reads Best? Factors Related to Reading Achievement in Grades 3, 7, and 11.* NAEP Report no. 17-R-01. Princeton, N.J.: Educational Testing Service, February 1988.

———, and Lynn B. Jenkins. *The Writing Report Card, 1984-88.* NAEP. Prepared by Educational Testing Service. Washington, D.C.: U.S. Department of Education, Office of Educational Research and Improvement, January 1990.

Astuto, Terry A., and David L. Clark. *The Effects of Federal Education Policy Changes on Policy and Program Development in State and Local Education Agencies.* Bloomington, Ind.: Policy Studies Center of the University Council for Educational Administration, March 1986.

Baker, Curtis O. *The Condition of Education: 1989.* Volume 1, *Elementary and Secondary Education.* Washington, D.C.: U.S. Government Printing Office, 1989.

Barton, Paul E. *Earning and Learning.* NAEP Report no. 17-WL-01. Princeton, N.J.: Educational Testing Service, March 1989.

Berryman, Sue E. *Breaking Out of the Circle: Rethinking Our Assumptions about Education and the Economy.* Occasional Paper no. 2. New York: Teachers College National Center on Education and Employment, July 1987.

———. "Seven Bottom Lines for Smarter Educational Reform." Presentation for the Fortune Magazine Education Summit, New York, Teachers College Institute on Education and the Economy, October 1989.

———. *Shadows in the Wings: The Next Educational Reform.* Occasional Paper no. 1. New York: Teachers College National Center on Education and Employment, March 1987.

Berrueta-Clement, J.R., L.J. Schweinhart, W.S. Barnett, A.E. Epstein, and D.P. Weikart. *Changed Lives: The Effects of the Perry Preschool Programs on Youths Through Age 19.* Ypsilanti, Mich.: High/Scope Press, 1984.

Branch, Alvia, Sally Leiderman, and Thomas J. Smith. *Youth Conservation and Service Corps: Findings from a National Assessment.* Philadelphia: Public/Private Ventures, December 1987.

Brookover, William, et al. *School Social Systems and Student Achievement.* New York: Praeger, 1979.

"The Care and Education of Young Children: Expanding Contexts, Sharpening Focus." *Teachers College Record* 90, no. 3 (Spring 1989). Special issue.

Chubb, John E., and Terry M. Moe. *Politics, Markets, and America's Schools.* Washington, D.C.: Brookings Institution, 1990.

Clune, William H., Paula White, and Janice Patterson. *The Implementation and Effects of High School Graduation Requirements: First Steps Toward Curricular Reform.* New Brunswick, N.J.: Rutgers Center for Policy Research in Education, February 1989.

Corcoran, Thomas B., Lisa J. Walker, and J. Lynne White. *Working in Urban Schools.* Washington, D.C.: Institute for Educational Leadership, 1988.

Cremin, Lawrence A. *Popular Education and Its Discontents.* New York: Harper and Row, 1990.

———. *Public Education.* New York: Basic Books, 1976.

Cuban, Larry. *The Managerial Imperative and the Practice of Leadership in Schools.* Albany, N.Y.: State University of New York Press, 1988.

Darling-Hammond, Linda. *Beyond the Commission Reports: The Coming Crisis in Teaching.* Santa Monica, Calif.: Rand Corporation, July 1984.

———, and Barnett Berry. *The Evolution of Teacher Policy.* Santa Monica, Calif.: Rand Corporation, March 1988.

David, Jane L., et al. *Restructuring in Progress: Lessons from Pioneering Districts.* Washington, D.C.: National Governors' Association, 1989.

Doyle, Denis P., and Terry W. Hartle. *Excellence in Education: The States Take Charge.* Washington, D.C.: American Enterprise Institute for Public Policy Research, 1985.

Edmonds, Ronald. "Effective Schools for the Urban Poor." *Educational Leadership* 37 (October 1979): 15-27.

Educational Achievement: Explanations and Implications of Recent Trends. Washington, D.C.: Congress of the United States, Congressional Budget Office, 1987.

Elmore, Richard F. *Early Experience in Restructuring Schools: Voices from the Field.* Washington, D.C.: National Governors' Association, 1988.

———, and Milbrey Wallin McLaughlin. *Steady Work: Policy, Practice, and the Reform of American Education.* Santa Monica, Calif.: Rand Corporation, 1988.

Firestone, William, Susan Fuhrman, and Michael Kirst. *An Overview of Education Reform Since 1983.* New Brunswick, N.J.: Rutgers Center for Policy Research in Education, March 1989.

———. *The Progress of Reform: An Appraisal of State Education Initiatives.* New Brunswick, N.J.: Rutgers Center for Policy Research in Education, October 1989.

Fox, James. *The Impact of Research on Education Policy.* Working Paper OR90-522. Washington, D.C.: Office of Educational Research and Improvement, U.S. Department of Education, March 1990.

General Accounting Office. *Education Reform: Initial Effects in Four School Districts.* GAO/PEMD-89-28. Washington, D.C.: U.S. General Accounting Office, September 1989.

Goodlad, John I. *What Schools Are For.* Bloomington, Ind.: Phi Delta Kappa Educational Foundation, 1979.

Grant, Gerald. *The World We Created at Hamilton High.* Cambridge, Mass.: Harvard University Press, 1988.

Gross, Beatrice, and Ronald Gross, eds. *The Great School Debate: Which Way for American Education?* New York: Touchstone, 1985.

Guthrie, James W., and Rodney J. Reed. *Educational Administration and Policy: Effective Leadership for American Schools.* Englewood Cliffs, N.J.: Prentice-Hall, 1986.

Gutman, Amy. *Democratic Education.* Princeton, N.J.: Princeton University Press, 1987.

Hannaway, Jane, and Robert Crowson, eds. *The Politics of Reforming School Administration.* New York: Falmer Press, 1989.

Hayward, Becky J., Nancy E. Adelman, and Richard N. Apling. *Exemplary Secondary Vocational Education: An Exploratory Study of Seven Programs.* Washington, D.C.: U.S. Department of Education, National Assessment of Vocational Education, February 1988.

Heath, Shirley Brice, and Milbrey Wallin McLaughlin. "A Child Resource Policy: Moving Beyond Dependence on School and Family." *Phi Delta Kappan* 68, no. 8 (April 1987): 576-580.

Hill, Paul T., Arthur E. Wise, and Leslie Shapiro. *Educational Progress: Cities Mobilize to Improve Their Schools.* Washington, D.C.: Rand Center for the Study of the Teaching Profession, January 1989.

Hodgkinson, Harold L. *All One System: Demographics of Education — Kindergarten through Graduate School.* Washington, D.C.: Institute for Educational Leadership, 1985.

Kaagan, Stephen S., and Richard J. Coley. *State Education Indicators: Measured Strides, Missing Steps.* Princeton, N.J.: Educational Testing Service, 1989.

Kagan, Sharon L., ed. *Early Care and Education: Reflecting on Options and Opportunities.* Special theme issue of *Phi Delta Kappan* 71, no. 2 (October 1989).

————, and Edward F. Zigler. *Early Schooling: The National Debate.* New Haven, Conn.: Yale University Press, 1987.

Kaplan, George. *Who Runs Our Schools: The Changing Face of Educational Leadership.* Washington, D.C.: Institute for Educational Leadership, 1989.

Kidder, Tracy. *Among Schoolchildren.* Boston: Houghton Mifflin Company, 1989.

Kirsh, Irwin S., and Ann Jungeblut. *Literacy: Profiles of America's Young Adults.* NAEP. Princeton, N.J.: Educational Testing Service, N.d.

Knapp, Michael S., and Brenda J. Turnbull. *Better Schooling for the Children of Poverty: Alternatives to Conventional Wisdom.* Volume 1, *Summary.* Washington, D.C.: U.S. Department of Education, January 1990.

Langer, Judith A., Arthur N. Applebee, Ina V.S. Mullis, and Mary A. Foertsch. *Learning to Read in Our Nation's Schools: Instruction and Achievement in 1988 at Grades 4, 8, and 12.* NAEP. Prepared by Educational Testing Service. Washington, D.C.: U.S. Department of Education, Office of Educational Research and Improvement, June 1990.

Lapointe, Archie E., Nancy A. Mead, and Gary W. Phillips. *A World of Differences: An International Assessment of Mathematics and Science.* Princeton, N.J.: Educational Testing Service, January 1989.

Lazerson, Marvin, Judith Block McLaughlin, Bruce McPherson, and Stephen K. Bailey. *An Education of Value: The Purposes and Practices of Schools.* New York: Cambridge University Press, 1985.

Levin, Henry M. "Cost-Effectiveness and Educational Policy." *Educational Evaluation and Policy Analysis* 10, no. 1 (Spring 1988): 51-69.

Lewis, Anne. *Restructuring America's Schools.* Arlington, Va.: American Association of School Administrators, 1989.

Lieberman, Ann, ed. *Building a Professional Culture in Schools.* New York: Teachers College Press, 1988.

————. *Rethinking School Improvement: Research, Craft, and Concept.* New York: Teachers College Press, 1986.

————. *Schools as Collaborative Cultures: Creating the Future Now.* New York: Falmer Press, 1990.

Lightfoot, Sarah Lawrence. *The Good High School: Portraits of Character and Culture.* New York: Basic Books, 1983.

Lortie, Dan C. *Schoolteacher: A Sociological Study.* Chicago: University of Chicago Press, 1975.

Maeroff, Gene I. *The Empowerment of Teachers: Overcoming the Crisis of Confidence.* New York: Teachers College Press, 1988.

Metz, Mary Haywood. *Different by Design: The Context and Character of Three Magnet Schools.* New York: Routledge and Kegan Paul, 1986.

Miller McNeill, Laurie. "The State Education Reform Movement and the Reform of the State Politics of Education." Ph.D. diss., Columbia University, 1989.

Mullis, Ina V.S., and Lynn B. Jenkins. *The Reading Report Card, 1987-88: Trends from the Nation's Report Card.* NAEP. Prepared by Educational Testing Service. Washington, D.C.: U.S. Department of Education, Office of Educational Research and Improvement, January 1990.

———. *The Science Report Card: Elements of Risk and Recovery.* NAEP Report no. 17-S-01. Princeton, N.J.: Educational Testing Service, September 1988.

Murnane, Richard J. "Education and the Productivity of the Work Force: Looking Ahead." In *American Living Standards: Threats and Challenges,* ed. Robert E. Litan, Robert Z. Lawrence, and Charles L. Schultze. Washington, D.C.: Brookings Institution, 1988.

Nathan, Joe, ed. *Public Schools by Choice: Expanding Opportunities for Parents, Students, and Teachers.* St. Paul, Minn.: Institute for Learning and Teaching, 1989.

Oakes, Jeannie. *Improving Inner-City Schools: Current Directions in Urban District Reform.* New Brunswick, N.J.: Rutgers Center for Policy Research in Education, October 1987.

———. *Keeping Track: How Schools Structure Inequality.* New Haven, Conn.: Yale University Press, 1985.

Office of Technology Assessment. *Informational Technology and Its Impact on American Education.* Washington, D.C.: U.S. Government Printing Office, 1982.

Papert, Seymour. *Mind-Storms: Children, Computers, and Powerful Ideas.* New York: Basic Books, 1980.

Passow, A. Harry. "Present and Future Directions in School Reform." Paper prepared for conference at Trinity University, San Antonio, Tex., August 18-21, 1987.

———. *Reforming Schools in the 1980s: A Critical Review of the National Reports.* New York: ERIC Clearinghouse on Urban Education, Teachers College, April 1984.

———."Whither (or Wither?) School Reform?" *Educational Administration Quarterly* 24 (1988): 246-256.

Peterson, Paul E. "Did the Education Commission Reports Say Anything?" *Brookings Review* 2 (Winter 1983): 3-11.

———. *The Politics of School Reform, 1870-1940.* Chicago: University of Chicago Press, 1985.

Popkewitz, Thomas S., B. Robert Tabachnick, and Gary Wehlage. *The Myth of Educational Reform: A Study of School Responses to a Program of Change.* Madison: University of Wisconsin Press, 1982.

Powell, Arthur G., Eleanor Farrar, and David K. Cohen. *The Shopping Mall High School: Winners and Losers in the Educational Marketplace.* Boston: Houghton Mifflin Company, 1985.

Public Schools of Choice. Alexandria, Va.: Association for Supervision and Curriculum Development, 1990.

Purkey, Stewart C., and Marshall S. Smith. "Effective Schools: A Review." *Elementary School Journal* 83 (March 1983): 427-452.

Ravitch, Diane. *The Schools We Deserve: Reflections on the Educational Crises of Our Time*. New York: Basic Books, 1985.

————. *The Troubled Crusade: American Education, 1945-1980*. New York: Basic Books, 1984.

————, and Chester E. Finn, Jr. *What Do Our 17-Year-Olds Know?: A Report on the First National Assessment of History and Literature*. New York: Harper and Row, 1987.

The Reading Report Card: Progress Toward Excellence in Our Schools. Trends in Reading over Four National Assessments, 1971-1984. NAEP Report no. 15-R-01. Princeton, N.J.: Educational Testing Service, N.d.

Reed, Sally, and R. Craig Sautter. "Children of Poverty: The Status of 12 Million Young Americans." *Phi Delta Kappan* 71, no. 10 (June 1990): K1-12.

Reingold, J.R., and Associates, Inc. *Current Federal Policies and Programs for Youth*. Washington, D.C.: William T. Grant Foundation Commission on Work, Family and Citizenship, June 1987.

Resnick, Lauren B. "Learning in School and Out." *Educational Researcher* 16, no. 9 (December 1987): 13-20.

Restructuring: What Is It? Special theme issue of *Educational Leadership* 47, no. 7 (April 1990).

Rodriguez, Richard. *Hunger of Memory: The Education of Richard Rodriquez*. New York: Bantam Books, 1982.

Rutter, Michael, Barbara Maughan, Peter Mortimore, Janet Ouston, and Alan Smith. *Fifteen Thousand Hours: Secondary Schools and Their Effects on Children*. Cambridge, Mass.: Harvard University Press, 1979.

Sarason, Seymour B. *The Culture of the School and the Problem of Change*. 2d ed. Boston: Allyn and Bacon, 1982.

School Boards: Strengthening Grass Roots Leadership. Washington, D.C.: Institute for Educational Leadership, November 1986.

School Dropouts: Everybody's Problem. Washington, D.C.: Institute for Educational Leadership, 1986.

School Dropouts: Survey of Local Programs. GAO/HRD-87-108. Washington, D.C.: U.S. General Accounting Office, July 1987.

Sedlak, Michael, and Steven L. Schlossman. *Who Will Teach? Historical Perspectives on the Changing Appeal of Teaching as a Profession*. Santa Monica, Calif.: Rand Corporation, November 1986.

Social Policy 15, no. 2 (Fall 1984). Special issue on school effectiveness.

Steiner, Gilbert Y. *The Children's Cause*. Washington, D.C.: Brookings Institution, 1976.

Stern, Joyce D., ed. *The Condition of Education: 1987 Edition*. Washington, D.C.: U.S. Government Printing Office, 1987.

52

———, and Mary Frase Williams, ed. *The Condition of Education: 1986 Edition.* Washington, D.C.: U.S. Government Printing Office, 1986.

Teaching in the Eighties: A Need to Change. Special issue of *Harvard Educational Review* 57, no. 1 (February 1987).

Trends in Educational Achievement. Washington, D.C.: Congress of the United States, Congressional Budget Office, 1986.

Tyack, David B. *The One Best System: A History of American Urban Education.* Cambridge, Mass.: Harvard University Press, 1974.

———, and Elisabeth Hansot. *Managers of Virtue: Public School Leadership in America, 1820-1980.* New York: Basic Books, 1982.

———."Hard Times, Then and Now: Public Schools in the 1930s and 1980s." *Harvard Education Review* 54, no. 1 (February 1984): 33-66.

Useem, Elizabeth L. *Low Tech Education in a High Tech World.* New York: Free Press, 1986.

Youth Indicators 1988: Trends in the Well-Being of American Youth. Washington, D.C.: U.S. Department of Education, Office of Educational Research and Improvement, August 1988.

Weick, Karl E. "Educational Organizations as Loosely Coupled Systems." *Administrative Science Quarterly* 21 (March 1976): 1-19.

Wetzel, James R. *American Youth: A Statistical Snapshot.* Washington, D.C.: William T. Grant Foundation Commission on Work, Family and Citizenship, June 1987.

What Americans Study. Princeton, N.J.: Educational Testing Service, 1989.

White Plisko, Valena. *The Condition of Education: 1984 Edition.* Washington, D.C.: U.S. Government Printing Office, 1984.

Wilson, William Julius. *The Truly Disadvantaged: The Inner City, the Underclass, and Public Policy.* Chicago: University of Chicago Press, 1987.

Wirt, John G., Lana D. Muraskin, David A. Goodwin, and Robert H. Meyer. *National Assessment of Vocational Education: Final Report.* Volume 1, *Summary of Findings and Recommendations.* Washington, D.C.: U.S. Department of Education, National Assessment of Vocational Education, July 1989.

Wise, Arthur E. *Legislated Learning: The Bureaucratization of the American Classroom.* Berkeley: University of California Press, 1979.

Work-Based Learning: Training America's Workers. Washington, D.C.: U.S. Department of Labor, Employment and Training Administration, November 1989